Global Food Insecurity

A Selective Annotated Bibliography of Dissertations and Theses

Grayson L. Parke

Parke, Grayson L.

Global Food Insecurity: A selective annotated bibliography of dissertations and theses/Grayson L. Parke

p. cm.

1. Food security – Social Aspects. 2. Hunger – Social Aspects. I. Title.

RA 65 .O23

362.196

ISBN-10 151524282X

ISBN-13 978-1515242826

Table of Contents

Global Food Insecurity

A Selective Annotated Bibliography of Dissertations and Theses

1.) **Abate, T. A.**

Government intervention and socioeconomic change in a northeast Ethiopian community: An anthropological study.

Ph.D. dissertation, Boston University. 2000.

This dissertation is a study of two rural development programs implemented by the Amhara regional state in South Wollo, Ethiopia. Based on two years of ethnographic fieldwork conducted between 1996-1998, the study examines the cultural and institutional constraints the government encountered in attempts to alleviate rural poverty and food insecurity by redistributing land more fairly among households and by disseminating improved agricultural techniques. Data collection methods employed in the study included formal and informal interviews, census data, questionnaire surveys and extensive participant observation. The dissertation argues that both programs have done more to promote dominant party control over rural peoples than to increase food security and agricultural productivity. The political and cultural dimensions of this are traced to the continuity of an elite attitude which portrays farmers as tradition-bound, inefficient and incapable of improving their lot without strong guidance from above. This was reinforced by deeply embedded cultural conceptions of power and authority where superiors and subordinates equate acquiescence with loyalty, and questions or suggestions with insubordination. It was further reinforced by the relatively dyadic and transitory nature of relations among household heads that prevented the formation of long-lasting mutual ties of cooperation among farmers. The dissertation demonstrates that at crucial stages of their implementation, both programs were characterized by unresolved contradictions between stated government objectives and the conflicting interests of politicians, bureaucrats and farmers at the district and local levels. The negotiations and struggles that occurred because of these contradictions had the effect of either preserving the status quo or transferring power to a new elite within a largely unchanged system. Meaningful attempts at structural change proved elusive in spite of government ideological proclamations to the contrary. The study argues that no improvements in the effectiveness of government programs will come about until these relationships are recognized as an integral part of the process and dealt with accordingly. [Author Abstract]

2.) **Acker, T.**

Measuring food insecurity in Guatemala.

Honors thesis, Ohio State University. 2011.

This thesis is an internal and criterion validation study on the Latin America and Caribbean Food Security scale (Escala Latinoamericana y Caribena de Seguridad Alimentaria - ELCSA) conducted in over 200,000 households in Guatemala. A fifteen-question survey was distributed in eight of the thirteen departments of Guatemala; from the indigenous western region, to the forested, impoverished northwest region....; Abstract: This thesis is an internal and criterion validation study on the Latin America and Caribbean Food Security scale (Escala Latinoamericana y Caribena de Seguridad Alimentaria - ELCSA) conducted in over 200,000 households in Guatemala. A fifteen-question survey was distributed in eight of the thirteen departments of Guatemala; from the indigenous western region, to the forested, impoverished northwest region. The eastern region was excluded. This study demonstrated the efficacy of the survey in measuring the severity of household food insecurity. The data were received from the Guatemala National Institute of Statistics and analyzed using the Rasch model to determine the survey's internal validity, through use of a severity scale and infit values. The criterion validity was supported through use of 1-way ANOVA and chi square statistics and demonstrated statistically-significantly correlations between the food insecurity status found in this study and other previously identified food insecurity factors. This study further documented the Latin American and Caribbean Food Security scale as an internally and externally valid instrument recommended for use in national representative surveys to measure household food insecurity. A valid and reliable tool to measure food insecurity is necessary to successfully target at-risk and high-risk populations and to efficiently implement and monitor interventions. [Author Abstract]

3.) **Adams, A. M.**

Seasonal food insecurity in the Sahel: nutritional, social and economic risk among Bamana agriculturalists in Mali.

Ph.D. dissertation, University of London, London School of Hygiene and Tropical Medicine (United Kingdom). 1992.

This thesis considers the nutritional, social and economic dimensions of seasonal food insecurity in Mali from the conceptual viewpoint of risk. It incorporates both longitudinal and cross-sectional designs, and quantitative and qualitative methods to explore the strategies agriculturalists employ to minimize risk, and the characteristics of the vulnerable. Anthropometry, morbidity, adult energy expenditure, and household food consumption were monitored over a 14 month period in a village sample of 33 households to test the hypothesis that seasonal nutritional risk is experienced differentially by age and gender groups in the population. Significant seasonal changes were detected in all nutritional indicators, but few which exceeded threshold levels used to define risk. At the household level, the thesis examines the hypothesis that exogenous factors and endogenous household characteristics combine to influence the range of strategies available to food insecure households, and therefore, the degree of risk they experience. Cross-sectional data on seven villages revealed striking interregional and interannual variations in the prevalence and severity of household food insecurity which are strongly related to rainfall. Household stratification according to the capacity to sustain a secure, adequate and viable diet revealed the food secure to be large and wealthy households, with sufficient resources to diversify production, and to invest in agriculture and social networks of exchange. At the other extreme were food insecure housholds which tend to be poor, small and dependent on the proceeds of labour sales to breach the shortage period. Longitudinal study of food stock flows, labour exchange, monetary expenditure and other transfers, demonstrated the continuing vitality of social networks of exchange as means of spreading risk. Vulnerable households had less access to such networks. [Author Abstract]

4.) **Adeigbe, R. T.**

The relationship between food insecurity and physical inactivity and the role of social support.

M.S. thesis, The University of Texas at San Antonio. 2012.

Currently 15% of the US population is food insecure. Food insecure individuals are shown to be less physically active, have less social support, higher rates of depression and are at higher risk for the development of chronic disease. Purpose: The purpose of the study was to investigate the relationships between food insecurity and physical inactivity and to determine if social support moderated this relationship. Research Focus: This study aimed to answer the following questions: (1) Is there a relationship between food insecurity and physical inactivity? (2) What are the correlates of physical inactivity and food insecurity? (3) Does social support moderate the relationship between food insecurity and physical activity? Methods: This was a cross sectional study using secondary data from the National Health and Nutrition Examination (NHANES) survey. The three main variables for this study were weekly physical activity minutes, food security status and social support. Demographic variables were used as correlates. A total of 2,307 cases were used for analysis. Independent sample t-test, linear regression, logistic regression, chi-square and moderated mediation analysis tests were ran to answer the studies research questions. Results: Independent t-test results found that food insecure individuals significantly participated in less physical activity compared to food secure individuals. Also, results of the regression analysis revealed income and education to be shared correlates between physical activity minutes per week, not meeting the PAGA and food insecurity. Gender, race, marital status and BMI were insignificant. Mediated moderation results revealed social support was not a moderator between food insecurity and physical activity. Discussion: Food insecure individuals tend to be younger than food secure individuals, have larger household sizes, less education and lower household incomes compared to food secure individuals. Food insecure individuals also participate in significantly less weekly physical activity and leisure time physical activity but more transportation and household physical activity compared to food secure individuals. Social support does not moderate the relationship seen between food insecurity and physical inactivity; however, literature supports the importance of social support in increasing physical activity levels. With increasing obesity rates, increased sedentary behaviors, more US adults not meeting the PAGA, and the highest rates of food insecurity in the past 15 years, understanding the characteristics of this food insecure population and potential factor contributing to physical inactivity can help structure interventions and programs to reduce chronic disease and improve the health of this population. [Author Abstract]

5.) **Agea, J. G.**

Use and potential of wild and semi-wild food plants in alleviating household poverty and food insecurity: a case study of Bunyoro-Kitara Kingdom, Uganda.

Ph.D. dissertation, University of Wales, Bangor (United Kingdom). 2010.

This study explored the use and potential of WSWFPs in alleviating household poverty and food insecurity in Bunyoro-Kitara Kingdom, Uganda. Specifically, it: (1) documented WSWFPs commonly consumed, parts consumed, contribution to the diet, cultural significance and social implications of their consumption by the local people; (2) explored the local methods of harvesting, preparation, and preservation of the commonly consumed WSWFPs; (3) assessed the nutritional values of selected WSWFPs; (4) assessed the market potential of the traded WSWFPs; (5) determined local management practices, selection criteria, constants, opportunities and strategies to use and management of WSWFPs in the Kingdom. Household survey using semi-structured questionnaire was used to collect data on the objectives 1 and 5. Focus group discussions (FDGs) were held to seek data on objective 2 and parts of objectives 1 and 5. Rapid market surveys (RMS) were conducted to collect data on objective 4. Field walks with key informants were conducted to collect samples of selected WSWFPs for laboratory analysis. Selection of WSWFPs for nutrient content analyses were guided by SWOT (strength, weakness, opportunities and threats) analysis in reference to availability of the plant, market value, available information on nutritional composition, and extent of anthropogenic pressure on species. Data from household survey, key informant interviews, FGDs and RMS were analysed using a combination of methods and statistical packages. The laboratory and analytical procedures included determination of moisture, ash, calories, protein, fat, total carbohydrates, dietary fibre, vitamins, essential macro, and micro mineral elements contents using standard procedures. [Author Abstract]

6.) **Alaimo, K.**

Consequences of food insufficiency for American children.

Ph.D. dissertation, Cornell University. 2000.

The research in this dissertation was undertaken to determine the health, cognitive, academic, psycho-social and anthropometric consequences associated with living in food insufficient families for American children. Data from the Third National Health and Nutrition Examination Survey were analyzed. For each category of outcomes, a theoretical model was created that described the relationships between family and child resources, food insufficiency, environmental risks, health care risks, past nutrition, health, and social risks, and the outcome of interest. Data were analyzed to determine associations between food insufficiency and the outcome, after adjusting for other factors in the model. Food-insufficient children ages 1--16 years were significantly more likely than food-sufficient children to have been reported in poorer health status after adjusting for potential confounding factors. Food-insufficient children were also more likely to have more frequent stomach aches, headaches, and, among pre-school children, more frequent colds. Furthermore, 6--11 year old food-insufficient children had lower arithmetic scores, and were more likely to have repeated a grade and seen a psychologist. Food-insufficient teenagers ages 12--16 years were almost two times as likely to have seen a psychologist, been suspended from school, and have difficulty getting along with other children, as compared to food-sufficient children. For 15--16 year old adolescents, after adjusting for socio-demographic characteristics, food insufficiency was significantly associated with dysthymia, having thoughts of death, having a desire to die, and having attempted suicide. Finally, food insufficiency was not significantly associated with being overweight. Food insufficiency was not the only important risk factor; family income was also significantly associated with many of the adverse outcomes studied. In addition, the number of other risks a child had, including such factors as low parental education, high blood lead concentration, and lack of health insurance was significantly associated with children's cognitive, academic and psycho-social outcomes. The results of this research demonstrate that negative health, academic and psycho-social outcomes are associated with family food insufficiency and provide support for public health efforts to increase the food security of American families. [Author Abstract]

7.) **Ansari, N. B.**

The role of household food insecurity access, socioeconomic status and dietary diversity as underlying determinants of undernutrition in Pakistani households.

Ph.D. dissertation, University of California, Davis. 2010.

Child undernutrition and food security are serious problems facing Pakistan, with almost 42% of children under five years being stunted and almost 50% being anemic. It is estimated that almost three-quarters of the Pakistani population live below the poverty line of $2 income per day, and although Pakistan is an agricultural economy, the real problem is not the availability of food but the lack of purchasing power of its citizens. Nearly one-half of Pakistan's population lack adequate income to purchase food required to meet their caloric needs. With household food insecurity as an underlying determinant of undernutrition, our first study's aim was to adapt and validate the global nine-question Household Food Insecurity Access Scale (HFIAS) version 3 for use in Pakistan. We concluded that the HFIAS was reflective of the three domains of food insecurity access (anxiety and uncertainty about the household food supply; inadequate food quality; and insufficient food intake), and could be used by policymakers and researchers to identify and target groups for food insecurity reduction programs. Even though socioeconomic status (SES) is considered a total measure of the economic and sociological position of a household and its members relative to others in society, there is little consensus in defining SES, especially in developing countries. Researchers collect a plethora of information to account for SES, but few studies efficiently utilize the information collected. As part of a project to demonstrate scaling-up of evidence-based nutrition interventions in Pakistan, we collected baseline data from nearly 47,000 households in a large district. Our study aim was to demonstrate the usefulness of principal component analysis in identifying useful SES indicators to develop a meaningful SES index in rural, periurban and urban areas of Pakistan. Contrary to our assumption, our index did not load heavily on tangible assets and/or the presence of livestock, even in rural areas, as some studies on health inequalities have shown. Instead, we found the largest variance was explained by the frequency of purchasing basic commodities of oil, sugar, tea and wheat, as well as the health-seeking behavior of children under five and pregnant women. Lastly, with strong evidence supporting the association of dietary diversity and improved nutritional status, we used Pakistan's National Nutrition Survey 2001-2002 to characterize dietary factors associated with anemia in young Pakistani children between 6 and 59 months of age. Our results confirmed that irrespective of age group, a majority of Pakistani children were being fed a monotonous diet, with only 22% meeting the recommendation to consume foods from at least four different food groups per day. We found an inverse relationship between the proportion of children consuming iron-rich sources of food and the severity of their anemia. After adjusting for the child's age, mean hemoglobin was significantly higher in children who consumed flesh foods versus those who did not (10.9 vs 10.6 g/dl, $p<0.05$) as well as for eggs (11.3 vs 10.6 g/dl, $p<0.001$). We also found a significant trend between severity of anemia and the lack of maternal knowledge regarding dietary sources of iron. In our final multivariate logistic regression model, children reportedly not consuming egg(s) or whose mother was unable to identify dark green leafy vegetables as a source of dietary iron were twice as likely to be anemic, after adjusting for the child's age. Our findings, in combination with the high rate of malnutrition among Pakistani children, should alert policymakers and health care personnel that left to their own means, Pakistani mothers may not be aware of the importance of iron-rich foods as well as which foods are an important source of iron. [Author Abstract]

8.) **Aranka, A.**

Relationship between food insecurity and HIV outcomes among individuals receiving antiretroviral therapy in British Columbia, Canada.

Ph.D. dissertation, University of British Columbia. 2012.

Little is known about the relationship between food insecurity and health outcomes among people living with HIV/AIDS. This dissertation therefore sought to: i) review global evidence regarding the associations between food insecurity and HIV outcomes; ii) assess the prevalence and correlates of food insecurity among HIV-positive individuals receiving antiretroviral therapy (ART) across British Columbia (BC); iii) examine the relationship between hunger and plasma HIV RNA suppression among illicit drug users receiving ART in Vancouver; and iv) investigate the potential impact of food insecurity on mortality among injection drug users (IDU) receiving ART in BC....; Background: Little is known about the relationship between food insecurity and health outcomes among people living with HIV/AIDS. This dissertation therefore sought to: i) review global evidence regarding the associations between food insecurity and HIV outcomes; ii) assess the prevalence and correlates of food insecurity among HIV-positive individuals receiving antiretroviral therapy (ART) across British Columbia (BC); iii) examine the relationship between hunger and plasma HIV RNA suppression among illicit drug users receiving ART in Vancouver; and iv) investigate the potential impact of food insecurity on mortality among injection drug users (IDU) receiving ART in BC. Methods: Adults receiving ART in three BC-based observational studies completed interviewer-administered surveys eliciting information about socio-demographic profile, risk behavior, and health status, and consenting to database linkage for retrieval of clinical, laboratory and prescription information. Explanatory, confounder and survival models were built to investigate the associations between food insecurity and ART outcomes. Results: A growing body of literature suggests that food insecurity is associated with increased risk of HIV transmission, poor ART access, adherence, pharmacokinetic efficacy, immunologic and virologic response, and reduced survival (Chapter 2). In a sample of 457 individuals receiving ART across BC, food insecurity was reported by 71% and was independently associated with younger age, illicit drug use, low annual income, tobacco smoking and symptoms of depression in explanatory models (Chapter 3). Among 406 illicit drug users receiving ART in Vancouver, 63% reported hunger and 59% had suppressed viral loads. Hunger and virologic suppression were not independently associated in multivariate confounder models (Chapter 4). Among 254 IDU receiving ART across BC, 41% died between June 1998 and September 2011. Food insecurity was associated with a two-fold increased risk of death. [Author Abstract]

9.) **Bas, J. A.**

Considering global food insecurity: The case of Cuba. A national alternative to the global capitalist food distribution system.

M.A. thesis, Dalhousie University (Canada). 2005.

This thesis explores Cuba's unique food security policy in order to evaluate whether the Cuban approach might be applicable in other contexts. The FAO estimates that there are 852 million hungry or starving people in the world (2004)---a fact which is all the more devastating given that there are enough food resources for everyone. The case of Cuba presents an example of a small third world nation which, prior to the collapse of the Soviet Union and Eastern European socialism (1989-1991), had eliminated malnutrition. Since then, Cuba has embarked on a radical redirection of agricultural and food policy, favouring small scale agricultural production, liberalization of a portion of the agricultural market, and sustainable agriculture in both rural and urban areas. This thesis finds that elements of Cuba's new agriculture and food policy have been successful and, therefore, the case of Cuba offers valuable lessons in food security. [Author Abstract]

10.) **Bengle, R. A.**

Food insecurity and cost-related medication non-adherence in a population of community-dwelling, low-income older adults in Georgia.

M.S. thesis, University of Georgia. 2009.

This study examined the relationship between food insecurity and cost-related medication non-adherence in a population of low-income older adults in Georgia. This study used data from the Georgia Advanced Performance Outcomes Measures Project to evaluate new Older Americans Act Nutrition Program participants and waitlisted people (n = 1000, mean age 75.0 ± 9.1 years, 68.4% women, 25.8% black). Food insecurity was assessed using the modified 6-item USDA Household Food Security Survey Module. Practice of 5 CRN behaviors (e.g., delaying refills, skipping doses) was evaluated. Approximately 49.7% of participants were food insecure, while 44.4% had utilized [greater than or equal to]1 CRN strategy (CRN-P). Those who were food insecure and/or who reported CRN-P were more likely to be black, low-income, younger, and less educated. After controlling for confounders, food insecure participants were 2.9 (95% CI 2.2, 4.0) times more likely to report CRN-P. Improving food security is important for low-income older adults to promote adherence to recommended prescription regimens. [Author Abstract]

11.) **Bitto, E. A.**

Poverty and food insecurity in rural Iowa: An examination of four food desert counties. Ph.D. dissertation, Iowa State University. 2005.

Pockets of poverty are found throughout rural Iowa. Rural America is comprised of people with varying backgrounds who much make their livelihoods in a society that is increasingly a part of a global village. Living in Iowa, called by many the breadbasket of the world, does not necessarily mean that everyone will have equal access to food. In fact, over 46,600 Iowans between 2001-2003 experienced some form of poverty and 9.4 percent were defined as food insecure. This dissertation examines the economic structure of Iowa's counties to determine how agriculture and local business influence per capita income, inequality, and poverty. One examination of how poverty impacts people is food insecurity. The study focuses on four Iowa counties defined as food deserts--places with four or fewer grocery stores. In these counties I find many individuals participating in the countermovement--the alternative market--across all income levels as people grow their own gardened food and share with family, neighbors and friends. Participating in the countermovement provides access to goods and services that individuals might otherwise not be able to economically afford. Data suggests that individuals who are food secure are more likely to participate in community organizations, be more socially connected, and more likely to participate in the countermovement. For communities, when the basic needs are completely met, people are more likely to become involved in community organizations and create a larger social capital base. Some research suggests that improvement in health care, nutrition, and housing will create a spill-over effect onto communities that can establish higher forms of social and financial capital as well as having a healthier community. [Author Abstract]

12.) **Bodnar, S.**

Competing needs: An exploration of major illness as a predictor of rising rates of food insecurity.

M.P.H. thesis, Yale University. 2010.

The prevalence of household food insecurity is the highest it's ever been since nationally representative food security surveys were first conducted in 1995 (Household Food Security in the United States, 2008). The cost of health care has been rising at a much faster rate than the growth in national income (Health Care Costs and Election 2008, Kaiser Family Foundation). More Americans are exposed to health care costs through either lack of health insurance, steeper deductibles, higher premiums, or bigger copayments. The parallel increase in healthcare costs and food insecurity indicates a possible relationship between these two factors. The primary focus was to explore the association between food insecurity and different aspects of financial events resulting from ill health. Key findings include: (1) Large out-of-pocket medical expenses and lost time from work due to illness or injury are significantly associated with increased food insecurity, but only when these events occur in the last six months of a household's measured food security status. This suggests households that experience these events have a heightened risk of increased food insecurity, but that this risk is temporary. (2) Avoiding obtaining healthcare due to cost is significantly associated with increased food insecurity in the last six months of a household's measured food security, as well as the previous twelve months before that. Both anxiety regarding cost of medical care, as well as the expectancy that there will be a dire need for future medical care, could affect how much money a household spends on food. (3) An inability to borrow money from family or friends to pay for medical expenses or other unexpected costs, and financial responsibility for children outside the home, are also associated with a higher risk of increased food insecurity. These findings have critical implications for both research and policy relating to food insecurity and healthcare, which are discussed in the conclusion. [Author Abstract]

13.) **Bowers, N. E.**

Examination of food insecurity among single-parent households utilizing services in Oktibbeha County, Mississippi.

M.S. thesis, Mississippi State University. 2002.

The purpose of this study was to compare the food security status of single parent and other households participating in agencies associated with the Oktibbeha County Council on Community Resources. Two hundred adults completed a questionnaire containing a series of adult and child food security questions. The major fording was that food insecurity and food insecurity with hunger existed among the adults and children, and was significantly greater for single parent households. Food insecurity in single parent households was 53.3% and food insecure with hunger was 32.7%. A significantly higher percentage of single parent families participated in the food stamp program and the WIC Program than for other families. However, the majority of the families classified as food insecure and food insecure with hunger were not participating in the food stamp program but were using other agencies for assistance. This study confirms the need for local assistance programs. [Author Abstract]

14.) **Braunstein, N. S.**

Diet, food insecurity and dental caries prevalence and severity in children ages 2--11. Ph.D. dissertation, Boston University. 2008.

Dental caries is the most common chronic childhood disease. The association of diet, food insecurity and caries is unknown. Objectives . To evaluate the associations of diet quality, food insecurity and caries prevalence and severity in children ages 2-11. To examine consistencies in associations between dietary quality indicators and dental caries status in young children in the National Health and Nutrition Examination Survey (NHANES). Methods . Children ages 2-5 (n=801) and 6-11 years (n=1097) from the 2001-2002 who had dental exam, food security, and diet data were studied. Logistic and linear regression was used to explore relationships between caries status and diet exposures and food security status, controlling for age, race, poverty, household smoking, dental visits and health insurance coverage. Diet quality indicators and dental caries status were compared between NHANES 2001-2002 and NHANES III [1988-1994] (n=4119). Results . Children ages 2-5 in the upper quartile of diet quality were 69% less likely to have early childhood caries (ECC) (OR 0.31, 95% CI 0.18, 0.56) compared with those in the lowest quartile. Young children living in food insecure households had higher caries prevalence than food secure children (38.2% vs. 23.0%, p =0.004) and a 1.8 greater odds of caries (95% CI 1.09, 2.97). In children ages 6-11, multiple linear regression models identified specific eating behaviors (total number of meals and snacks, soda consumption and number of days/week school lunch eaten) as being significantly associated with the number of decayed and filled primary teeth (dft) ($p < 0.05$). Dietary quality and food security were not associated with dft or the number of decayed, missing and filled permanent teeth (DMFT). In children 2-5 years, there were consistent relationships in both NHANES 2001-2002 and III between ECC and the following dietary characteristics: total HEI score and its fruit, grain and cholesterol components; daily servings of vegetables, fruit, milk, yogurt and total dairy; and number of daily meals and soda consumption ($p < 0.05$). Conclusion . The association between diet quality, food insecurity and caries in children ages 2-5 and between dietary behavior and caries severity in older children have implications for public health policy and health promotion initiatives. [Author Abstract]

15.) **Browder, D. E.**

Latino mothers in rural America: A mixed methods assessment of maternal depression. Ph.D. dissertation, Iowa State University. 2011.

This dissertation examined depression among rural Latino women using two studies--one using quantitative methodologies and another using mixed methods design. Data were from a multi-state longitudinal project that tracked the well-being and functioning of low income rural families in the context of welfare reform. For one study, latent growth curve modeling (LGC) was used to test for moderation of race/ethnicity on the relationship between food security status, social service use, and depressive symptoms. For the other study, chi-square and t-test analyses were used to test for differences between two groups of Latino women--those who maintained a consistently low level of depressive symptoms and those who maintained a consistently high level of depressive symptoms. Also, qualitative analyses were used to determine commonalities and differences among those same groups of Latino women. The data showed that factors that influenced depression were complex and multi-faceted. The latent growth curve modeling showed that ethnicity moderated the relationship between food insecurity status and depressive symptoms with higher initial levels of food insecurity associated with higher initial levels of depressive symptoms. Using qualitative inquiry in a mixed methods design shed light on the mothers who maintained low depressive symptoms throughout this longitudinal study and highlighted the significance that one's family of origin has throughout life, specifically how a caring and supportive relationship with one's parents and siblings appears to buffer an individual from life's difficult circumstances and thus safeguard one's mental health. A meaningful extension of this dissertation would be to focus on the influence of family of origin on levels of depression and food security later in life. Further work needs to consider differing patterns of association with food insecurity and maternal depression based on earlier familial relationships and child outcomes. [Author Abstract]

16.) **Brown, N. L.**

Starved: Food deserts in the Mississippi delta.

M.A. thesis, The University of Mississippi. 2011.

This thesis examines the impact of food deserts on obesity, and builds a case for additional research on rural food deserts independent from urban ones. The Mississippi Delta consistently presents the highest obesity rates within the state, yet both the third unhealthiest county (Quitman) and the healthiest (DeSoto) are located in that region. One of the reasons there is such a large discrepancy between the health rankings of DeSoto and Quitman counties is that DeSoto is contained within the Greater Memphis Metropolitan Area, but Quitman is entirely rural. Previous research has focused on the prevalence of urban food deserts and resulted in scattered support from corporations like CVS and Walgreens to increase access to fresh fruits and vegetables; but the characteristics of urban food deserts and the solutions that are effective in resolving them are not always applicable to rural areas, where corporate presence is often limited to fast food restaurants. Using case studies of these two counties, this thesis identifies the challenges that are specific to rural food deserts and presents potential solutions. [Author Abstract]

17.) **Brown, S. S.**

Unavailable and inaccessible an analysis of urban food insecurity.

M.S. thesis, Virginia Commonwealth University. 2012.

This study explored food insecurity by examining the ways in which residents of low-income, urban communities access food. The primary elements of this thesis are an analysis of the demographic and socioeconomic characteristics of the populations surrounding food retailers, and a survey of the availability, cost, and quality of fresh fruits and vegetables in food stores commonly found in the urban environment. Overall, this study found that low-income, minority communities are largely served by independent supermarkets, small grocers and convenience stores that charge higher prices for staple foods. Conversely, it was found that wealthy areas enjoy easy access to corporate supermarkets that offer higher-quality foods at lower prices. [Author Abstract]

18.) **Bryceson, D. F.**

Food insecurity and the social division of labour in Tanzania, 1919-1985.

D.Phil. dissertation, University of Oxford (United Kingdom). 1988.

This thesis analyzes the socio-economic consequences of the Tanzania population's exposure to food insecurity between 1919 and 1985. The thesis covers: the incidence of food inadequacy in peasant households throughout the country; the impact of famine relief measures of the colonial state and the Native Authorities; the role of Asian traders; the development of an African wage labour force and its food demand; the problems of supplying food to plantation workers and other geographically dispersed wage labourers during the inter-war period; state food policies arising from the exigencies of World War II; decolonisation and the restructuring of the social division of labour on a non-radical basis between 1950 and 1973; state food production and marketing policy in response to rapid urban growth; African marketing cooperatives; the national economic crisis years between 1973 and 1985; the parastatalisation of national marketed food supply; the parallel food market; the state's difficulties in implementing its industrialisation and peasant agricultural transformation policies; and the deterioration of the functional division of labour to the extent that the occupational division of labour between rural and urban areas blurs. The central argument of the thesis is that food insecurity retards development of functional social groups and the organisational structure of the market and state relative to the household and clientage networks. This situation arises from the prevalence of risk-averting, household-based strategies of all functional groups in contradistinction to the maximizing strategies of market and state agents. With domination of household and clientage networks, the formation of functional groups is restricted to that made possible by face-to-face accountability or household ties. A circular process begins. Food insecurity is perpetuated and often intensified by the limited scale of the division of labour, its barriers to outside innovation and to the free flow of food between deficit and surplus areas through market channels. In the process, the technological development of food production is severely hindered. [Author Abstract]

19.) **Buchthal, O. V.**

The role of social capital in changing dietary behavior in a low-income multi-ethnic community.

Ph.D. dissertation, University of Hawai'i at Manoa. 2012.

Poor dietary quality contributes to health disparities experienced by low-income populations. Although prior studies have examined factors shaping dietary behavior among individual ethnic groups, there is little knowledge about structural factors shaping dietary decisions within multi-ethnic low-income communities. Low-income households have fewer resources for purchasing healthy food, and greater demands on the economic, time and labor resources required for meal preparation. With limited economic resources, families may rely on social capital resources to manage food within the household. However, social capital structures within a multi-ethnic community are likely to be complex. This dissertation explores the role of social capital in shaping dietary behavior in a multi-ethnic low-income Asian and Pacific Islander community in Hawai`i. The first study presents findings from a systematic literature review on the operationalization of social capital theory in nutrition research. This review identifies the primary theories of social capital underlying nutrition research, and the measures of social capital commonly used in this research. The second and third studies report on empirical research conducted in Kalihi, a low-income multi-ethnic neighborhood of Honolulu, Hawai`i. The second study uses qualitative methods to understand the dimensions of social capital within the community, and the ways that social capital affects household nutrition behaviors. The third study uses network analysis to assesses linkages between community organizations, mapping the structure of institutional social capital within the community. Together, these studies suggest that families in low-income multi-ethnic communities rely on social capital to provide resource for nutrition, and this reliance shapes dietary behavior. Social capital structures within this community, however, do not fit the theory and measures of social capital most commonly used in nutrition research. Improved theory and measure selection would strengthen the utility of social capital theory as a tool for understanding nutrition behavior. Individual social capital operates through extended family and ethnic group ties, not neighborhood geography. Access to bridging capital was primarily through family connections with childcare and faith-based institutions, but churches were poorly connected in the nutrition network. Building institutional social capital through increasing linkage between these organizations could provide support for improved nutrition across the community. [Author Abstract]

20.) **Bukhari, H.**

Food insecurity in the UK and its association with deprivation and attitude: The consequence on dietary patterns using diet quality index and BMI class.

Ph.D. dissertation, University of Southampton (United Kingdom). 2006.

This thesis is based on a secondary analysis of data to examine social and demographic aspects of food insecurity in Britain. The central hypothesis addresses the interaction between deprivation and negative attitudes and levels of food insecurity. The primary hypothesis was that greater food insecurity would lead to a lower diet quality characterised by a greater consumption of high energy food which in turn would lead to adverse changes in body composition. The worst off group was suggested to be those who are food insecure with deprivation and negative attitudes to healthy eating. The study is a pilot cross-sectional secondary analysis of an existing data set from a very deprived area in Leeds (459 households). The USA food insecurity short form questionnaire was used to measure the level of food insecurity. Information was collected on food consumption, on attitude towards healthy eating and sociodemographic variables. SPSS version 12 was used to analyse the data. The results showed that one in three households food insecure and the risk was three times more for the most deprived households with negative attitude to healthy eating. Food insecurity was associated with younger age, being female, being heavy smoking, being poorly educated and receipt of benefits for a prolonged time. The food insecure had a significantly lower score in a simplified diet quality index (DQI). Although food insecurity was not significantly related to body mass index (BMI), there was a trend to obesity and weight loss in the food insecure. However, analysis of the interaction of food insecurity, BMI and DQI showed a trend to low diet quality in all BMI classes of the food insecure that was significant only in the overweight group. Food insecurity is only one of the important factors which affect behaviour towards healthy eating and food choice. The results and trends in this study reinforce the need to investigate food insecurity further in the general population and the deprived communities in other cities. The recommendations from this pilot study for programs addressing food insecurity are to consider the possible interaction of variables that affect the perception of being food insecure in the UK. The nutritional consequences should be investigated further by using a fully validated DQI that evaluates the deficiency or excess in the major nutrients reported to be associated with food insecurity. [Author Abstract]

21.) **Calhoun, M. D.**

Food Insecurity in Urban and Rural Settings: A Mixed Methods Analysis of Risk Factors and Health.

Ph.D. dissertation, University of Ottawa (Canada). 2013.

Food insecurity exists when access to safe, nutritionally adequate foods is limited or uncertain, or when acquisition of these foods occurs in socially unacceptable ways (Anderson, 1990). Considerable research has focused on identifying the risk factors for and potential consequences of household food insecurity; however, few studies have investigated whether and how place of residence might influence household food insecurity. To address this gap in the literature, a mixed methods approach was used to explore the connections between risk factors, household food insecurity, and health in urban and rural settings. This dissertation comprised three studies. In the first study, secondary data were used to identify the household factors that increased the risk for household food insecurity and to examine whether place of residence moderated these relationships. Significant associations were found between household sociodemographics and household food insecurity. In addition, rural households were more likely to report household food insecurity. Although most moderation models were non-significant, a moderation effect was found for educational attainment: secondary school graduation increased the risk for household food insecurity in urban households, yet it was protective in rural households. In the second study, secondary data were used to examine the relationship between household food insecurity and poor general, physical, and mental health, and to test for a moderation effect of place of residence. In the main effects models, household food insecurity was associated with an increased likelihood of poor health on all measures. There was no evidence of urban-rural differences in these relationships. In the third study, qualitative data were used to explore household food insecurity from the perspective of urban and rural residents in Eastern Ontario. Findings revealed that urban and rural residents described similar conditions, processes, and consequences of household food insecurity; however, the unique features of the urban and rural settings influenced how people managed these experiences. In particular, certain aspects of the rural settings added to the complexity of managing household food insecurity. Overall, the results of this dissertation suggest that the urban-rural context, although important, is secondary to the primary contribution of low economic and social resources in household food insecurity. [Author Abstract]

22.) **Carmichael, L. L.**

Feast or famine trade distortions and food insecurity in developing states.

M.A. thesis, University of Georgia. 2010.

Food insecurity is defined as a situation that exists when people lack physical, social and economic access to sufficient, safe and nutritious food that meets their dietary needs and food preferences for an active and healthy life (FAO 2000). With eighty percent of the world currently residing in the less developed states and more than 95 percent of the world population increase expected in these states in the next decade, further attention to problem of food insecurity must focus on the developing world. What causes food insecurity in developing states? Current literature offers several explanations for food insecurity including: low production levels, natural disasters, and policies that discourage agricultural trade. This thesis: builds upon the political economic literature, argues that agricultural trade policies may lead to food insecurity, and uses data from the World Bank and FAO from 1990 to 2004 to test the current explanations for food insecurity. The research findings suggest that agricultural trade policies must be taken into account when determining whether food insecurity is likely to increase in a given state. [Author Abstract]

23.) **Carney, M. A.**

The Other Side of Hunger: Everyday Experiences of Mexican and Central American Migrant Women with Food Insecurity in Santa Barbara County.

Ph.D. dissertation, University of California, Santa Barbara. 2012.

This dissertation examines food insecurity in the context of displacement and transnational migration of women from Mexico and Central America to the US. Drawing upon 18 months of ethnographic fieldwork conducted between 2008 and 2011 in the coastal region of Santa Barbara, California, I advance and contribute to several arguments. In presenting the lived experience of "food insecurity," I analyze the everyday forms of structural violence that shape the experience of migrant women, particularly in terms of food, health, and bodies, and I critique interventions to food insecurity and "diet-related health problems" implemented by state and nonprofit agencies. I argue that through their everyday struggles and interactions with groups providing assistance, migrant women navigate power differentials rooted in distinctions of race, class, gender, and legal status while also negotiating and performing new modes of citizenship. Using data from participant observation, surveys, semi-structured interviews, life history interviews, and focus groups, I seek to answer the following research questions: What is the lived experience of food insecurity among Mexican and Central American migrant women in the US, and what are the structural forces contributing to this experience? At the local level, how do nonprofit entities and public health practitioners engage in the discourse and practice of food security, particularly as it affects migrant women? And, what do the lived experience of food insecurity and interventions by state and non-state actors reveal about changing notions of rights and citizenship and about the production of class and structural violence? The answers to these questions help inform my engagement with and contribution to four primary bodies of scholarship: political economy of food and migration; political ecology of food and health; ideas of power, the state, and hegemony; and critical approaches to race, class, gender, and citizenship. In engaging with the core themes of this dissertation--food, health, and citizenship--I analyze the dialectical relationship between structural conditions and individual agency. I use the rhetoric of "the other side" (el otro lado), a phrase invoked by migrant women to reference life outside of the US (specifically on the other side of the US-Mexico border), to underscore the variety of borders that limit access to livelihood resources for unauthorized migrants living in the US. [Author Abstract]

24.) **Carter, M. A.**

Do childhood excess weight and family food insecurity share common risk factors in the local environment? An examination using a Quebec birth cohort.

Ph.D. dissertation, University of Ottawa (Canada). 2013.

Background: Childhood excess weight and family food insecurity are food-system related public health problems that exist in Canada. Since both relate to issues of food accessibility and availability, which have elements of "place," they may share common risk factors in the local environment that are amenable to intervention. In this area of research, the literature derives mostly from a US context, and there is a dearth of high quality evidence, specifically from longitudinal studies. Objectives: The main objectives of this thesis were to examine the adjusted associations between the place factors: material deprivation, social deprivation, social cohesion, disorder, and living location, with change in child BMI Z-score and with change in family food insecurity status in a Canadian cohort of children. Methods: The Québec Longitudinal Study of Child Development was used to meet the main objectives of this thesis. Response data from six collection cycles (4 - 10 years of age) were used in three main analyses. The first analysis examined change in child BMI Z-score as a function of the place factors using mixed models regression. The second analysis examined change in child BMI Z-score as a function of place factors using group-based trajectory modeling. The third and final analysis examined change in family food insecurity status as a function of the place factors using generalized estimating equations. Results: Social deprivation, social cohesion and disorder were strongly and positively associated with family food insecurity, increasing the odds by 45-76%. These place factors, on the other hand, were not consistently associated with child weight status. Material deprivation was not important for either outcome, except for a slight positive association in the mixed models analysis of child weight status. Living location was not important in explaining family food insecurity. On the other hand, it was associated with child weight status in both analyses, but the nature of the relationship is still unclear. Conclusions: Results do not suggest that addressing similar place factors may alleviate both child excess weight and family food insecurity. More high quality longitudinal and experimental studies are needed to clarify relationships between the local environment and child weight status and family food insecurity. [Author Abstract]

25.) **Chakravarty, S.**

Harvesting health: Fertilizer, nutrition and AIDS treatment in Kenya.

Ph.D. dissertation, Columbia University. 2009.

This thesis explores various policy options for mitigating food insecurity among patients receiving treatment for HIV/AIDS. The first chapter examines the impact of a fertilizer provision program that targets farming households in which one or more members is currently receiving treatment for AIDS. The study enrolled 540 patients, of which half were selected to receive free fertilizer for the 2007 planting season. I find that treated households planted a larger acreage and produced 350 more kilograms of maize than control households, an increase of 40% worth about 88 USD. Treated households used the increased income from crop sales to invest in livestock and purchase 80% more fertilizer than the control group in the subsequent planting season. The second chapter extends the analysis of the impact of the fertilizer program to examine health outcomes of program participants. Fertilizer recipients, who concurrently received free anti-retroviral therapy (ART), experienced significant health improvements. Fertilizer provision improved the health status of treated individuals, as measured by both body mass index (BMI) and CD4 cell count. In the third chapter, I examine the impact of direct food distribution on the clinical outcomes of patients receiving ART at one clinic within the USAID-AMPATH partnership in western Kenya. The nutrition supplementation program began in 2004 and targeted patients with low Body Mass Index (BMI) and severe immunological suppression, as measured by CD4 cell count. Of the 1977 patients who initiated ART at this clinic, 548 participated in the food supplementation program. Results indicate that while both groups respond equally well to ART, the addition of food does not appear to significantly improve the outcomes of food recipients over the first 18 months of treatment. However, these results must be interpreted with caution due to the small sample size of CD4 and BMI measurements beyond the first 6 months of treatment. More rigorous evaluation, preferably with experimental design, of the impact of nutrition programs on the health outcomes of ART patients is needed. [Author Abstract]

26.) **Chalgian, E. R.**

Addressing food insecurity and developing social resources through community garden projects in low-income areas qualitative interviews with outreach coordinators from three urban agriculture organizations.

B.S. thesis, University of Montana. 2011.

As urban agriculture organizations become increasingly popular, it is important to understand the impact they have on low-income urban communities. Food security and political power are greatly lacking in these areas. Agriculture endeavors, such as community gardens and urban farms, have a significant potential to decrease these deficits. First, this thesis will address how social inequalities, which are products of structural power, prevent the poor from being properly fed and discuss how urban agriculture programs, specifically community gardens, can reduce food insecurity and build a community's social resources. Later, the discussion will focus on how low-income populations become involved in community agriculture projects. This latter discussion will be based on ethnographic interviews done with urban agriculture organization outreach coordinators who work with low-income communities. [Author Abstract]

27.) **Cherel-Robson, M. C.**

Vulnerability to food insecurity in Madagascar: spatial determinants, policy process and coping strategies.

D.Phil. dissertation, University of Sussex (United Kingdom). 2008.

There is a large body of literature on the conceptualisation of food security, but there has been little empirical investigation of its contextual characteristics and root causes. This thesis attempts to fill the gap by looking at the case of Madagascar. It utilises an interdisciplinary methodology based on an adaptation of the livelihoods framework to food security analysis.

Vulnerability is due to poverty, unfavourable natural endowments, and exposure to weather shocks, price fluctuations as well as idiosyncratic crises. Although Madagascar is ranked among the worst performers in Sub-Saharan Africa in terms of nutrition indicators, food security has consistently failed to become a top political priority. Limited public action is partly explained by the lack of pressure from civil society and fractionalisation amongst the key feed security actors within national institutions and donor agencies. The implications of the paucity of public safety nets were most evident after the 2002 politico-economic crisis. Limited livelihood options forced households to rely on asset depleting coping strategies as well as informal solidarity networks. However, the Fivahanana; the traditional myth of solidarity has been weakened by the hardship brought by successive crises. Increased uncertainty and changing times resulted in a growing individualism among the better off whereas the poor maintained traditional values of dignity and the accompanying costly customary obligations. Most of them failed to cope.

Conceptually, the study calls for a re-examination of dominant definitions of subjective food security. These definitions generally emphasis respect for local food preferences. What are the power dynamics behind the setting of these food preferences? Are these preferences consistent with objectives of good nutritional practices? Furthermore, the findings on the lack of primacy of food security in policy-making show the need for more research on unpacking local political and social constraints to eradicating food insecurity. [Author Abstract]

28.) **Coates, J. C.**

Mixed-method approaches to measuring the experience of food insecurity in Bangladesh and other developing countries.

Ph.D. dissertation, Tufts University. 2006.

This study investigated the nature of household food insecurity in Bangladesh and beyond, whom it affects and how, and the best methods for developing and validating scales to measure it in any culture. The following questions were examined in three separate papers: (1) How does a qualitatively-derived food insecurity scale compare to a scale developed using a quantitative approach? (2) To what extent and why do males and females in the same households respond differently to food insecurity questions? (3) What are the commonalities in the experience of food insecurity across cultures, and what are the implications for a generic or universal measure of food insecurity? The data were derived from the Bangladesh Food Insecurity Measurement and Validation study and supplemented by secondary data from 15 other countries. Key findings of the individual studies included: (1) The qualitatively and quantitatively derived scales were functionally equivalent, but the comparison of methods suggested that the statistical (Rasch model) approach used to develop food insecurity scales in the US and elsewhere should be reconsidered. (2) The rate of discordance in male and female responses to food insecurity questions ranged for individual items from 1% to 53%. Women and men responded differently to the same food insecurity questions because they had separate spheres of responsibility within the same household, there were power imbalances influencing intra-household food allocation, and the psychological responsibility for ensuring the household food supply was assumed by men more often than by women. (3) There is a common core to the food insecurity experience that transcends culture and that can be used as the basis for measuring the experience of food insecurity in any population. However, population sub-groups and individual households vary in how they manage these common elements of the problem. Preferences and practices, social acceptability, and the accessibility of food insecurity response options may explain variations in specific household responses to food insecurity. This research provides a theoretical and practical basis for developing and using functional measures of household food insecurity that are reflective of people's own experience of the problem while being cost-effective and easy to apply. [Author Abstract]

29.) **Cole, S. M.**

Exploring models of economic inequality and the impact on mental and physical health outcomes in rural Eastern Province, Zambia.

Ph.D. dissertation, The University of Arizona. 2012.

Structural adjustment measures adopted during the early 1990s considerably altered the rural landscape throughout Zambia. Households responded and continue to respond in a variety of ways, although many do so under highly inequitable terms. Poverty rates, food insecurity, and income inequality all remain unacceptably high in Zambia, particularly in rural areas. Using a biocultural and livelihoods approach, this alternate "publication in scholarly journals" format dissertation examines some of the complexities that condition livelihoods and differentially shape biologies in rural Zambia today. Three main problems are explored: 1) the relationship between food insecurity and adult mental health; 2) piecework (casual labor) as a coping strategy and indicator of household vulnerability to food insecurity; and 3) the association between relative deprivation and adult physical health. Research for the dissertation took place in a rural area in Eastern Province, Zambia in 2009. The research employed a mixed methodology, collecting qualitative and household-level survey data during the rainy and dry seasons. Various statistical analyses were utilized in the three papers appended to the dissertation. The results were further explored using the findings from the qualitative data. In paper one, a positive relationship between food insecurity and poor mental health was found. Food insecurity during the dry season had a greater effect on mental health than in the rainy season. In paper two, the results demonstrate the importance of piecework labor as a coping strategy and the need to adopt a multi-period lens to robustly assess whether participation in piecework reflects a household's vulnerability to food insecurity. In the third paper, a negative association was established between relative deprivation and adult nutritional status. Together, the results from the dissertation provide clear evidence that both the material and relative circumstances of people play important roles in patterning variation in mental and physical health outcomes in rural Zambia. [Author Abstract]

30.) **Coleman-Jensen, A. J.**

Time poverty, work characteristics and the transition to food insecurity among low-income households.

Ph.D. dissertation, The Pennsylvania State University. 2009.

Food insecurity refers to a household's inability to provide adequate food for all adults and children. This study focuses on how work characteristics--number of hours worked, schedule of employment, and commuting distance--relate to the transition to food insecurity. It is theorized that availability of time for household food provisioning will be reduced by certain job characteristics. Inadequate time for food provisioning and other household tasks--time poverty--will likely increase the amount of money households spend on food. These increases in expenditures may increase the likelihood of transitioning to food insecurity among low-income households. Much food insecurity research has been cross-sectional; this study is unique in analyzing a panel data set utilizing discrete time Event History analysis to model the first observed transition to food insecurity. Data for the study come from the Family Life Project, a sample of low-income households with young children from nonmetropolitan and small metropolitan counties that are followed over three years of data collection. The results suggest that households with mothers working full-time are more likely to become food insecure than households with mothers not working, controlling for income and other characteristics. Role overload, or greater demands on mothers' time, is significantly related to households transitioning into food insecurity. The theoretical framework developed, suggesting that time for food provisioning is a vital resource that can reduce the likelihood of becoming food insecure, is supported by the Event History analysis. Theories regarding time availability and allocation have not before been applied to understand how food insecurity develops. This research provides an important theoretical and substantive contribution to the food insecurity literature in documenting the importance of time as a resource affecting households' transitions to food insecurity. [Author Abstract]

31.) **Cooper, E. E.**

Hunger of the body, hunger of the mind: The experience of food insecurity in rural, non-peninsular Malaysia.

Ph.D. dissertation, University of South Florida. 2009.

Supplementary feeding continues to be a widespread strategy for child health promotion though its efficacy remains contested. The long-standing, Malaysian national food assistance program for children--Program Pemulihan Kanak-Kanak Kekurangan Zat Makanan (PPKZM)--fits this pattern, receiving severe criticism for its limited impact on child nutritional status. Still, the program remains, producing a seeming paradox and prompting questions of how it fits into (1) the larger political context of national health policy and (2) more localized village and clinic environments. This research combines historical inquiry with the in-depth, ethnographic study of two predominantly Malay coastal villages in Malaysian Borneo, where child anthropometry and household food insecurity rates establish a clear need for the PPKZM despite low coverage rates. This study assesses the ways in which common, local foods are perceived and categorized and the degree to which these understandings are shared both (1) within the communities and (2) between the communities and the clinics that serve them. Community members do not share a single core set of well-known food items. Instead, multiple microenvironments within the fieldsites likely dictate differential diets and prioritize distinct sets of foods. Agreement is more pronounced among clinic workers, who display a simple food classification system based almost exclusively on taxonomic differences with the rationale for these distinctions expressed in nutritional terms. Although community members recognize the same constitutive kinds, their categories are more nuanced and reflect the concerns of day-to-day practice, encompassing when and how a food item is encountered; its origins, relative expense, and common usage; and who will likely consume it. The dissertation relates cultural models for food classification to health education messages, PPKZM programming guidelines, community conditions, and food beliefs and practices. It facilitates an understanding of place--as viewed through the lens of food security--and addresses the relative fit of current nutritional programming within this context. The study offers concrete design recommendations for a successful, child-specific food package in the short-term while arguing for a more holistic, household-level solution. [Author Abstract]

32.) **Corbridge, T.**

Food Security Among Families with Children with Special Health Care Needs.

M.A. thesis, University of Washington. 2013.

Purpose: In 2012, 16.7 million (20.6%) of U.S. children lived in food-insecure households. Objectives of this study were to examine the association between household food security and presence of children with special health care needs (CSHCN) in a university-based pediatric dental clinic. Methods: Caregivers of patients under 18 years (n=142) at the University of Washington's Center for Pediatric Dentistry were surveyed about food security and CSHCN in their households. Results: Among households with CSHCN, 37% were food-insecure compared to 26% of households without CSHCN. Households with CSHCN with more health consequences had 2.59 higher odds of experiencing food insecurity compared to those without (95% CI 1.17, 5.72, p=0.019). This relationship was not significant after adjusting for covariates. Among households with CSHCN, those that were food-insecure reported significantly higher service use, functional limitations and need or use of mental health counseling in their CSHCN. Conclusions: Screening at dental visits identified a high proportion of families with food insecurity, particularly among some families with CSHCN. Screening for food insecurity may improve identification of needed services for children and their families. [Author Abstract]

33.) **Cowherd, R. E.**

The Effects of Food Insecurity on Mental Wellbeing in Monteverde Costa Rica. M.A. thesis, University of South Florida. 2012.

The rapid expansion of ecotourism in the Monteverde zone of Costa Rica has increased the incidence in food insecurity in the area. Changes in food preferences and availability have led to a more homogenized diet that is increasingly delocalized and reliant on processed foods. Additionally, there has been a rapid economic shift away from agricultural and dairy farming to an economy more reliant on tourism. This NSF supported study builds upon data from a longitudinal investigation (#BNS 0753017) examining the nutritional effects of this rapid economic transition. Using a mixed methods approach, a culturally appropriate scale of stress was developed and used in conjunction with the Household Food Insecurity Access Scale, the Cohen Perceived Stress Scale, and the Hopkins Symptom Check List to explore the relationship between food insecurity and mental health among residents of the Monteverde zone. Quantitative results show that food insecurity correlated positively with stress, depression and anxiety, and was found to be a significant predictor of stress and depression. [Author Abstract]

34.) **Cui, S.**

Dynamics of food insecurity of families with children.

M.S. thesis, Iowa State University. 2007.

Guided by family ecological theory, this paper empirically explored how family demographic, socioeconomic, and community characteristics, as well as public and government factors, are related to changes in a family's food insecurity status. Using 2001 and 2003 data from the Panel Study of Income Dynamics (PSID), a multinomial logit model of food security status was estimated. About 33.16% of the families with children under age 18 that were food insecure in 2001 became food secure in 2003. Meanwhile, about 4.48% of the families who were food secure in 2001 became food insecure in 2003. Although the average food insecurity of families changed only slightly between 2001 and 2003, the status of individual families changed substantially. This report, a first examination of the dynamic interdependence of food insecurity and a variety of family ecological characteristics over time, demonstrates the critical contribution of changing family circumstances to food insecurity. [Author Abstract]

35.) **De Marco, M. M.**

The relationship between income and food insecurity: The role of social support among rural and urban Oregonians.

Ph.D. dissertation, Oregon State University. 2007.

Millions of U.S. households experienced hunger in 2005 and millions more experienced food insecurity. Previous research indicates that low-wage work and little social support contribute to food insecurity. Research also suggests that individuals cope by finding alternate food sources and drawing on social support. Further, researchers have found that rural residents face difficulties that many urbanites do not, including lack of living-wage jobs, transportation, and nutrition assistance. However, rural dwellers may possess support they can leverage in difficult times. This study used mixed methods (i.e., quantitative and qualitative) to examine whether social support moderates the relationship between income and food insecurity and whether place of residence affects social support. First, a mail survey was conducted with a stratified random sample of Oregonians (n=343, 34.4% response rate). Subsequently, qualitative interviews (n = 25) were conducted with low-income or food insecure survey respondents to provide insight into these issues. Quantitative results indicate that lower income respondents were more likely to experience food insecurity. In general, social support did not moderate the relationship between income and food insecurity. When income was categorized using poverty guidelines, however, results suggested that emotional support, social network support, and organization membership may moderate this relationship. Specifically, respondents with incomes of ≤$19,999 were less likely to experience food insecurity in the presence of this support. However, small sample sizes in the ≤$19,999 income category resulted in unstable estimates of odds ratios (e.g., 4136.79). When income was recategorized to remedy this, the moderation disappeared. Additionally, place of residence had a significant association with only one social support measure, social network density. Rural respondents had less dense social networks than urban respondents. Place of residence was not a significant predictor of amount of social support via multivariate analysis. Several food insecurity contributors emerged from the qualitative study phase including ill health, unemployment, and having other expenses. Participants cited coping strategies such as use of alternate food sources, use of nutrition assistance, and drawing on social support. Although few significant quantitative results were found, qualitative findings suggest that developing nutrition interventions that build social support may lead to reduced food insecurity. [Author Abstract]

36.) **De Matteis, A.**

Market analysis to assist selection between response options in conditions of food insecurity.

Ph.D. dissertation, University of East Anglia. 2010.

Markets are key elements of people's livelihood both in normal conditions and in the immediate aftermath of a disaster, as long as markets function properly. Such recognition has contributed to the progressive acceptance of cash-based instruments and, more generally, to the strategic shift from food aid to food assistance with particular reference to cash transfers. However, such a shift has highlighted new needs, mainly in the form of analytical skills required to optimize the analysis of response options and support strategic decision making. Lack of capacity in this respect may be a critical constraint in the initial stages of emergency response.

This study has proposed and applied a few tools to assess the feasibility of cash transfers and to support the selection of intervention strategy. This has been done by assessing the functionality of markets and simulating the response of recipients and traders to an eventual cash-based intervention. Particular attention has been provided to the simulation of supply response. This is motivated by the consideration that when demand is artificially increased through cash transfers, much of the final outcome is determined by the capacity to scale up local supply. The profiling exercise of traders

conducted through the case studies has provided interesting behavioural information. In particular, how much price increases trigger traders' decision to scale up their business size has been investigated. Price rises generate a range of responses from different types of traders in different contexts, highlighting the need to define response capacity at local level. From this contextualized perspective the comparison between increased demand and supply has been used to estimate the price increase that can be expected from a certain injection of cash transfer to a set number of beneficiaries. [Author Abstract]

37.) **Devereux, S.**

Household responses to food insecurity in northeastern Ghana.

D.Phil., University of Oxford (United Kingdom). 1992.

When grain production falls short of consumption expectations in self-provisioning households, a range of responses is possible. How each household selects from and manages these responses provides the theoretical and empirical focus of this thesis. Several problematic issues in the `coping strategies´ literature are addressed, including questions of response sequencing and `discrete stages,´ the timing of asset sales for food, and the relationship between consumption protecting and consumption modifying strategies. Among other theoretical advances, criteria for response sequencing are identified which explain decisions about which assets to sell for food, and when, in terms of each asset's expected return rather than its immediate `entitlement´ value. This thesis is grounded in fieldwork conducted in the West African semi-arid tropics, a region characterised by seasonality, agricultural risk and market imperfections. Drought and armyworms undermined crop production in the fieldwork village in 1987/8. The community is highly stratified economically, and striking cross-sectional contrasts in household behaviour and nutritional outcomes were observed. Food secure households practice demographic, agronomic and economic diversification, which provide access to sources of food and income that are not correlated to local economic fluctuations. Consumption insecure households have narrower options and respond to production deficits by wealth depletion (asset monetisation, debt acquisition) and severe food rationing. Responses to production deficits are not confined to strategies for acquiring food. Multiple objectives - economic, nutritional and social - are retained. Nutritional adjustments are motivated by intertemporal economic priorities. The poorest households protected their assets and rationed consumption most severely: the cost of consuming resources rises as the number and value of assets owned falls. Within households, nutritional surveillance revealed that adults rationed their food consumption earlier and more severely than their children. Adult anthropometric status may therefore be a more robust predictor of food insecurity and economic stress than child anthropometry. [Author Abstract]

38.) **DeWitt, K. T.**

SNAP redemption at farmers' markets: A food systems approach to program implementation.

M.A. thesis, College of Charleston. 2013.

There is an emerging consensus among public health practitioners and policymakers alike that, given the existence of shared risk factors, the treatment of food insecurity and obesity requires integrated research and policy action. Referred to as the food systems approach , this perspective applies an ecological public health model for the conceptualization of the shared food environments from which food insecurity and obesity stem, and identifies opportunities for intervention centered on the promotion of healthy and sustainable food systems. One such food systems-based intervention that has garnered significant support is the redemption of the Supplemental Nutrition Assistance Program (SNAP) benefits at farmers' markets. However, the vast majority of studies that have examined the implementation of SNAP at farmers' markets have been conducted within a single market and have been designed to measure program impact, rather than the contextual determinants of program adoption and success. This study operationalizes the food systems approach and ecological model in order to examine the relationship between the implementation of SNAP at farmers' markets and macro-level physical food environment characteristics. Results indicate that the prevalence of SNAP-authorized farmers' markets is positively related to food system characteristics relating to local food production and distribution. The findings of this study contribute to the legitimacy of the food system approach and its application of an ecological public health model in the identification, formulation, and implementation of interventions designed to combat food insecurity and obesity. When enriched by the science of food environment assessment and measurement, the ecological model employed by the food systems approach provides a suitable framework for the systematic analysis of the macro-environmental context in which food systems-based interventions are implemented. [Author Abstract]

39.) **Ding, M.**

Food Insecurity and Undiagnosed Chronic Conditions among Adults.

M.S. thesis, Auburn University. 2012.

The purpose of this thesis is to examine the relationship between food insecurity and undiagnosed chronic conditions, including prediabetes, hypertension and hyperlipidemia, among adults (20-64y). Food security status was assessed by the ten items for adults from Food Security Survey Module. Undiagnosed chronic conditions were determined by comparing self-reported information with clinical examination evidence. The clinical definition for prediabetes was fasting plasma glucose = 100-125 mg/dl or A1C =5.7-6.4%, for hypertension was blood pressure 9Æ 140/90 mm Hg, and hyperlipidemia was defined by several criteria, including triglyceride, LDL, HDL and total cholesterol. Food insecure adults were more likely to have undiagnosed prediabetes (odds ratio 1.49, 95% CI 1.17-1.88). The relationship between food insecurity and undiagnosed hypertension and hyperlipidemia no longer existed after adjusting for confounding variables. These results indicate that food insecure adults may not know their risk status for diabetes. Screening for diabetes in food insecure populations appears to be warranted. [Author Abstract]

40.) **Dinh, A. M.**

Effects of Food Insecurity on Fast Food Consumption A Cross Sectional Study.

M.S. thesis, University of Washington. 2012.

The purposes of this study were: (1) to document the prevalence of food insecurity in a university based pediatric dentistry clinic, (2) to describe factors related to food insecurity, and (3) to determine the association between food insecurity and fast food consumption. Methods: English-speaking parents/ caregivers of children presenting for dental care at The Center for Pediatric Dentistry (CPD) in Seattle (WA) were recruited (N=212). Caregivers completed a 36-item survey, which included a validated USDA food security questionnaire. Descriptive statistics were determined for all variables. T-tests and Chi-square tests were used to test associations between food insecurity and fast food consumption. Logistic regression with robust variance estimation was used to further evaluate this association between food insecurity and fast food consumption after adjusting for potential confounders. In addition, multivariate logistic regression with robust variance estimates was used to determine associations with covariates of interest and fast food consumption. Results:. Two hundred twelve subjects participated in this study. The mean age was 39.7 years (SD = 9.7). The majority was female (77%), White (58%), born in the United States (69%), married (56%), and had public dental insurance (63%) Almost half (46%) had some college education or vocational training. Twenty seven percent had an annual income of more than $50,000. Twenty-eight percent of the families were food insecure. After adjusting for these covariates, the following factors were significantly associated with food insecurity: loss of job (OR=3.82, 95% CI =1.24-11.76), poor mental health status (OR=2.58, 95% CI=1.09-6.10), housing insecurity (OR=3.01, 95% CI=1.22-7.44) and annual household income p=0.007. After adjusting for the covariates, public dental insurance became significantly associated with fast food consumption (OR=0.33, 95% CI=0.13-0.84). There was no statistically significant association between food insecurity and fast food consumption (p=0.531). Conclusions: The prevalence of food insecure households was 28% at CPD. Factors associated with insecurity included: housing instability, lost job within the last year, poor mental health, and income. There was no statistically significant association between food insecurity and fast food consumption. [Author Abstract]

41.) **Djabatey, R. L.**

Agro-climatic hazards and the political economy of food insecurity in West Africa: A case of a rural food economy.

M.A. thesis, Wilfrid Laurier University (Canada). 1993.

Variability and declining food production and accessibility in West Africa have characterised the food system in the region's rural economy. These phenomenon have contributed to the fluctuation and declining per capita food supply and calorie intake, falling wages of farmers, rising food prices and increasing reliance on food imports and food aid by the governments and people of West Africa. The cause of the problem still remains an illusion and continues to baffle policy makers. Very often the problem is attributed to drought. However, to reduce the problem of household food insecurity to natural forces is to miss the centre of the issue and to exonerate political and economic institutions that, both by omission and commission, play significant roles in creating this unfortunate situation. Based on research information available for this study, this author is of strong conviction that political, economic and social factors are potent agents underlying household food insecurity in West Africa. Thus, one of the significant findings of the research is that, drought or food availability decline are not the potent factors responsible for food crisis in the study area. Rather, the breakdown of traditional coping mechanisms and entitlement failure (due to loss of income and rising food price) are responsible for household food insecurity in the study area. Furthermore, the research revealed that food crisis is not impacted on rural households with equal intensity. That is to say, there are differences in the impact of food crisis among various occupational households, and even among household members. Based on the research findings, the author recommends among others, the need to preserve and enhance local coping mechanisms, as well as to initiate development programmes that seek to channel investment resources to local farmers, and enhance the entitlement capacity of the rural people. The participation of the local people, especially women, in decision-making in regards to the designing, management, monitoring, and evaluating of food security measures were also recommended. [Author Abstract]

42.) **Doocy, S. C.**

Recurrent drought in Ethiopia: Microfinance programs as a means of improving coping capacity.

Ph.D. dissertation, The Johns Hopkins University. 2004.

This study evaluated the impact of the WISDOM microfinance program on household coping capacity and well being in drought-affected regions of Ethiopia. The study assessed the effect of microfinance programs on household income, savings, assets, diet, nutritional status, and coping capacity. A three-group cross-sectional design was used comparing established clients to two comparison groups, incoming clients and community controls. The 819 household survey was executed in May 2003 in two branches of WISDOM in the states of Oromiya and South Nations, Nationalities and Peoples Region. Microfinance participation resulted in diversification of income. Clients reported significantly more income sources than incoming clients or community controls ($p < 0.05$ for both comparisons) and significantly more income sources per economically active individual in the household ($p < 0.05$ for both comparisons). In the primary survey site, Sodo, wasting malnutrition rates in female clients and their children were significantly lower than in comparison groups. The odds of wasting in female controls as compared to female clients ranged from 3.2 (95% CI: 1.1-9.8; WHO recommendations) to 5.5 (95% CI: 0.9-58.8; NHANES reference standard) depending on the cutoff applied. Children of male clients and community controls, respectively, were 2.0 and 2.1 times more likely to be moderately or severely wasted than children of female clients

(95% CI: 0.95-4.41 for male clients and 95% CI: 1.00-4.61 for community controls). As compared to female clients, male clients and community controls were, respectively, 1.94 (95% CI: 1.05-3.66) and 2.08 (95% CI: 1.10-4.00) times more likely to have received food aid during the past year. That female clients and their children had enhanced nutritional status and were less likely to be recipients of food aid suggests differential effects of participation in lending programs by client sex where program impact is greatest among female clients. Findings of this study suggest that microfinance programs are successful in increasing household coping capacity in chronic natural disasters, especially when clients are female, and indicate that microfinance programs may have an important role as a means of enhancing population well being in the context of natural disasters and humanitarian emergencies. [Author Abstract]

43.) **Doudna, K. D.**

The longitudinal relations between depression and parenting self-efficacy in rural mothers with low incomes.

M.S. thesis, Iowa State University. 2012.

This thesis examined depression and parenting self-efficacy in context with individual and family variables, in two different studies. Data were aggregated from a multi-state, longitudinal research project that examined the effects of the 1996 welfare reform on the functioning and well-being of rural families with low household incomes. Both studies used path analysis to determine the relations between variables, and test for moderation effects. The first study examined relations between food insecurity, depression, parenting self-efficacy and perceived parenting support, with knowledge of community resources acting as a moderator. The second study examined relations between depression, parenting self-efficacy and family functioning, with financial pressure as a moderator. The results showed that depression and food insecurity predict each other over time, and that depression negatively affects parenting self-efficacy, perceived parenting support, and family functioning. Knowledge of community resources and financial pressure were found to be moderators of specific paths in the models. These results suggest that rural families with low income, especially those who experience financial pressure, would benefit from mental health services that address maternal depression within the context of the family. Additionally, since depression and food insecurity are linked, mental health professionals should consider making families aware of food assistance programs for which they may qualify, and food assistance program personnel may consider partnering with mental health professionals. [Author Abstract]

44.) **Eicher-Miller, H.**

The association of food insecurity to health and dietary outcomes in U.S. children.

Ph.D. dissertation, Purdue University. 2009.

Food insecurity, a condition associated with decreased nutrient intake and poor health, may eventually lead to negative health outcomes in children, including iron deficiency, iron deficiency anemia, and a low bone mass accumulation. The purpose of this study was to formally investigate the relationship of food insecurity to iron and calcium related health outcomes in U.S. children, 3-19y (n=11,247) and 8-19y (n=6,252) respectively. Participants of the National Health and Nutrition Examination Survey 1999-2004 were classified for food security status using the US Children's Food Security Scale and the US Household Food Security Scale in a cross-sectional study completed in homes and National Health and Nutrition Examination Survey Mobil Examination Centers across the United States. Iron deficiency was classified by two or more abnormal values for transferrin saturation, serum ferritin, erythrocyte protoporphyrin with the addition of abnormal hemoglobin to classify iron deficiency anemia. Bone mineral content was determined with whole body dual-energy x-ray absorptiometry. Dietary measures were quantified by 24-hour dietary recall. The odds of iron deficiency anemia among children 12-15y were 2.95 (CI: 1.18-7.37) times more likely (P =0.02) for children in households with food insecurity among children compared with children in households with food security among children. Males 8-11y from households with food insecurity among children had an estimated lower total body (52.5g ±21.7g), head (11.2g ±4.6g) lumbar spine (1.6g ±0.7g), left arm (4.3g ±1.6g), and left leg (11.3g ±5.8g) BMC compared with males from households with food security among children. Health disparities persist among food insecure children. The results of this study indicate a continuing need for successful interventions to reduce iron deficiency anemia, to improve bone health among food insecure children, and to reduce food insecurity among U.S. children. [Author Abstract]

45.) **El Obeid, A. E. T.**

Political institutions and chronic food insecurity in developing countries: An empirical analysis.

Ph.D. dissertation, Iowa State University. 2001.

World food production is growing at a faster rate than population growth and capita food energy has increased in developing countries. However, approximately 800 million people in the developing world still do not have access to sufficient food for an adequate diet. An additional quarter of a billion people periodically face food inaccessibility due to weather, instability in prices and employment, drought, diseases and civil strife, Furthermore, the distribution of food is uneven around the world. There have been a number of theses advanced on why millions of people around the world go hungry including poverty, rapid population and urban growth, uneven distribution of food, inadequate domestic agricultural production, trade barriers and inappropriate macroeconomic policies leading to negative or slow economic growth. However, an important factor that has not been investigated is the relationship between food insecurity and the political institutions in developing countries. The objective of this study is to better understand the sources of food security problems in developing countries and to explore empirically the strength of selected factors in explaining the underlying reasons for food security problems. The study provides an empirical analysis of the causes of chronic food insecurity including the much ignored political, civil and economic freedoms. A cross-sectional econometric model is used with data from 153 developed and developing countries for the period 1995. The empirical analysis assesses the relative importance of the factors hypothesized to explain the differences among countries for a widely used indicator of food insecurity. The indicator of food insecurity, per capita dietary energy supply, is regressed on selected economic variables including measures of political rights and civil liberties, and economic freedom. The results show that political rights and civil liberties impact food security in developing countries indirectly through income. Countries that enjoy political and civil freedoms tend to enjoy higher incomes and in turn, are more food-secure than countries where these freedoms are repressed. These results suggest that the institutions of developing countries, which underlie these rights or freedoms, are critical in the design of interventions to alleviate poverty and therefore, food insecurity. [Author Abstract]

46.) **Fantry, R.**

Fresh food access and lower-income populations in the Charleston, SC tri-county area. M.P.A. thesis, College of Charleston. 2011.

South Carolina is currently second in the nation in hunger. As rates of public and private food assistance program utilization have risen, lower-income populations have been left behind in the movement towards organic and local fresh food economies and utilization. For these populations, the acquisition of any food is the priority. This causes lower-income populations to possibly experience health problems due to the cheaper and easier to acquire nature of energy-dense, high calorie foods versus more expensive, harder to acquire fresh food options. Several organizations in the Charleston tri-county area are focused on bridging the gap for these lower-income populations, providing more access to fresh food grown in the lowcountry. Case studies of three organizations: Fields to Families, Metanoia Community Development Corporation, and the Lowcountry Food Bank examine how each organization meets this need, gaps in service, and desired changes and support to improve access and organization success. [Author Abstract]

47.) **Feder, L. R.**

Reducing food insecurity among low-income pregnant women by providing community-based food resource information.

Ph.D. dissertation, Temple University. 2001.

Although nutrition education programs for pregnant women have produced favorable outcomes, they have been less successful in improving the quality of maternal diets, and have not explicitly addressed food insecurity. The purpose of this study was to measure the extent of food insecurity among a clinical population of low-income pregnant women, and to assess the impact of an educational approach to reduce food insecurity on the quality of maternal diets. The subjects were 180 inner-city, adult, pregnant women at a hospital-based prenatal clinic. Subjects were enrolled over a ten-month period. Each one-week period was randomly assigned to receive either (a) standard nutrition education (comparison group) or (b) a standard nutrition education plus community-based food resource information, in the form of an educational handout (intervention group). A questionnaire was used to assess food security status, diet quality, use of community-based food programs and resources, and barriers to utilizing food resources. A follow-up questionnaire was completed by 119 (66%) of the women. The results showed that 65% of the baseline sample indicated food insecurity. Food insecure women had less education, were less likely to shop at supermarkets, and were more likely to cite barriers to obtaining food than food secure women. Level of food insecurity was significantly negatively correlated with fruit and vegetable intake, and was positively correlated with age and the total number of barriers. Both at baseline and at follow-up, there were no significant differences between the study groups for food insecurity, diet quality, or utilization of food programs and resources. At follow-up, the comparison group was significantly more likely to cite two of the barriers than the intervention group. Therefore, it was concluded that the educational intervention had no measurable impact on food insecurity, diet quality, or utilization of food resources, and minimal, if any, impact on the barriers. It is recommended that future research focus on those women with the highest levels of food insecurity, and that pregnancy might not be the optimal time for intervention. Also, food security scales could be used as screening tools in clinical settings, so that food insecurity is addressed during nutrition education. [Author Abstract]

48.) **Ferrer, M. C.**

Three essays on food environment, health and nutrition, and food insecurity.

Ph.D. dissertation, University of Georgia. 2012.

This dissertation consists of three essays on health, nutrition and food security programs. The research objectives include identification and explanation of the complex interrelationship between food insecurity, health and nutrition, and several food environment factors. More specifically, the socio-economic factors associated with government food-assistance programs and obesity/diabetes rates in the U.S. were analyzed in this study. The data included county-level observations taken primarily from the Food Environment Atlas and other secondary sources for 2006 and 2008. Poverty was the major determinant of food insecurity, health and nutrition issues, and the food environment. In the first essay, factors associated with obesity and diabetes were analyzed using county data throughout the U.S. The results suggest that local food structures are associated with reduced diet-related diseases; however, it is not a stand-alone solution to the problem. Other determining factors include education, diet, milk/soda price ratio, access to healthy food products, availability of recreational facilities, race/ethnicity, age, and poverty. In the second essay, household food insecurity as reflected in participation rates in the Supplemental Nutritional Assistance Program (SNAP) was analyzed at national and regional levels. County poverty rates and socio-economic indicators such as income levels, unemployment rates, education, and food deserts are explanatory factors associated with household food insecurity. National programs aimed at mitigating food insecurity rates are definitely helpful; however, a regional and more specialized approach tailored to the need of each area may improve responses to food insecurity. In the third essay, the analysis looks at food insecurity in children as it is manifested in National School Lunch Program (NSLP) participation rates. Median household income and unemployment rate are consistently significant explanatory variables of childhood food insecurity, before and during the recession, both at the national and regional models. Consistent with the results from the second essay, education, and food deserts are other factors associated with food insecurity in children. [Author Abstract]

49.) **Gebre, Y. D.**

Population displacement and food insecurity in Ethiopia: Resettlement, settlers, and hosts.

Ph.D. dissertation, University of Florida. 2001.

In the 1980s, the Ethiopian government relocated about 600,000 people from drought-affected and over-populated regions. Over 82,000 settlers moved to Metekel, a place occupied by the Gumz people. The official objective of the resettlement was preventing famine and attaining food security. Settlers recruited in late 1984 and early 1985 welcomed relocation, while those enlisted after mid-1985 were forcibly removed. The study explored (1) whether voluntary and forced migrations could be discriminated clearly, (2) the reasons for differential responses to forced migration, (3) the relationship between resettlement and food security, and (4) the effects of the resettlement on the hosts. The study, conducted in 1998 and 1999, employing interviews, surveys, and other techniques revealed (1) the migration behavior of settlers, including the act of embracing forced relocation, reflected the contexts and sets of relationships in which people found themselves; (2) the voluntary and forced settlers differentially readjusted in the Metekel; and (3) the host population sustained an irretrievable disruption due to the resettlement. [Author Abstract]

50.) **Geddis, A. M.**

School administrators' use of the National School Lunch Program to address the needs of students living in poverty.

Ed.D. dissertation, University of Illinois at Urbana-Champaign. 2012.

According to a 2007 U.S. Census report, 43% of children in America younger than six are classified as low income (U.S. Census Bureau, 2007). The USDA (2008a, 2009a) indicated 17.1% of school-aged children are classified as overweight; an additional 15% are at risk of becoming overweight; and approximately 17.2 million children are living in food- insecure households. Nationwide, poverty, obesity, and food insecurity are harsh realities for school-aged children. The state of Illinois is not exempt from these problems. With poverty, obesity, and food insecurity challenging the daily lives of children, schools should be empowered to meet some of these challenges. The purpose of this qualitative inquiry was to investigate how elementary school district administrators in south suburban Chicago school districts implement the National School Lunch Program and examine how they maximize the nutrition provided to children who live with poverty. This research sought to describe the lived experiences of the administrators who are given charge over the National School Lunch Program and develop meaning from these experiences. Consistent with research, this study found that school administrators who work in high poverty schools tend to prefer such settings, and conveyed a sense of purpose in their work. This study found that while they minimized their efforts, these school administrators were shining examples of transformative leaders who were taking steps to address the issues of food insecurity and obesity for children. Researchers estimate that it costs about one to three times as much to educate students from disadvantaged communities compared to more advantaged communities (Wall, 2006). It appears that the same is true for feeding children in disadvantaged communities. This study revealed that the overall food service expenses for these high poverty districts greatly exceeded the expenditures made in districts serving Illinois' most affluent neighborhoods. The School Nutrition Dietary Assessment Study III (USDA, 2007) indicated that over two-thirds of the public school lunches did not meet the USDA requirements for total fat or saturated fats. As the meals analyzed in this study consistently failed to meet the calorie and other nutrient benchmarks, it is evident that we must educate and provide solutions for those most responsible for the school menu. As the administrators in this study expressed their hopes and desires to serve their students more nutritious meals, I believe these transformative leaders have stumbled upon a solution that can address issues of obesity, food insecurity, and some of the economic conditions for the communities in which they serve. [Author Abstract]

51.) **Geida, J. A.**

Maternal depression affects maternal eating behaviors as shown by levels of disinhibition, food insecurity, and perceived barriers to healthy eating in a sample of WIC mothers.

Honors thesis, Pennsylvania State University. 2012.

One in 10 mothers is depressed in the United States. Depression impacts a mother's ability to care for herself and others. Additionally, low-income mothers are often food insecure and nutritionally deprived. The purpose of this study is to understand the prevalence of depression among low-income mothers enrolled in WIC of birth to two years, examine the relationship between depression and restraint/disinhibition, and to investigate how depression is associated with perceived levels of food insecurity and barriers to healthy eating. Methods: The study consisted of a cross-section of 60 low-income mothers enrolled in central Pennsylvania's WIC program. Mothers completed the Eating Inventory to assess restraint and disinhibited eating, Food Insecurity Screen and View of Family Meals questionnaire, Barriers to Healthy Eating Survey (BHES), and the Center for Epidemiological Studies Depression Scale (CES-D Scale). Height and weight were self-reported. Results: The majority of mothers were white (75%), unemployed (50%), and had annual incomes below the poverty level (46%); 37% were clinically depressed. Depressed mothers were significantly less likely to engage in disinhibited eating and more likely to report higher levels of dislike for healthy foods and difficulties attaining healthy foods contributing to higher total barriers to healthy eating ($p<0.05$). Depressed mothers also reported higher levels of food insecurity ($p<0.5$). There was no significant relationship between depression and restraint or maternal BMI ($Pr>0.15$). Conclusions: The proportion of mothers who were clinically depressed was 3.6 times higher than the national average and was associated with lower levels of disinhibited eating, higher barriers to healthy eating, and higher reported food insecurity. Depression also has adverse effects on mother's parenting abilities such as reducing responsive parenting and responsive feeding, leading to poor outcomes for the child. In future WIC intervention programs, depression treatment through counseling or support groups and the importance of consuming a healthy diet should be addressed to ensure that depressed mothers engage in healthy eating practices and do not face unnecessary struggles with parenting. [Author Abstract]

52.) **Girvent Muncunill, C.**

Food insecurity in Orange County: reasons for the underutilization of the Food Stamp program by Latino households.

D.P.A. thesis, University of La Verne. 2011.

This is a dissertation about food insecurity in the Latino population of Orange County, California, and the reasons for their underutilization of the Food Stamp program according to themselves. Problem Statement. Latino households living under the poverty level and experiencing food insecurity are underutilizing the Food Stamp program. Purpose: To contribute to knowledge that can affect practice in public administration and thus address the needs of society, namely, the living conditions of Latinos in Orange County. Theoretical Framework. This study is supported by three main theories: interpretivism, social constructionism, and social stratification. These foundational theories need to be seen as general tendencies, not absolute orientations. Methodology: This is a descriptive case study that utilizes a multistrategy quantitative and qualitative research method. It includes extensive secondary data and the collection of primary data in food pantries through structured observation and self-administered questionnaire instrument. Findings: The barriers to getting Food Stamps most commonly cited by Latinos have to do with myths and incorrect assumptions about the program followed by access or logistics issues. In a third position are barriers related to programmatic concerns and last are personal reasons. Latinos overwhelmingly cited immigration issues as a barrier. Promotion of the program in the observed food pantries is mostly nonexistent.

Conclusion and Recommendations: The role of government is recognized as essential to ensure people's access to basic needs. Poverty and its common consequence, food insecurity, need to be addressed with justice, not charity. Ending hunger in the United States requires the political will to address socioeconomic inequalities and the replacement of the minimum wage for the livable wage. New proactive approaches to make the Food Stamp program more accessible are urgently needed. The strong reliance on community by Latinos requires a new operational model in which Food Stamps case workers become community workers who interact with Latinos in public spaces. Given the low level of awareness and incorrect assumptions about the program, public campaigns should be expanded in mainstream media outlets; and most importantly for the underserved Latino community, all in need who qualify should be included regardless of their immigration status. [Author Abstract]

53.) **Goetz, J. R.**

Exploring food insecurity among individuals with serious mental illness: A qualitative study.

Ph.D. dissertation, University of Kansas. 2008.

Individuals with serious mental illness (SMI) are likely highly vulnerable to food insecurity, yet this issue remains unexplored within this population. Methods. A mixed method approach to assess the prevalence and underlying factors was conducted. Food security status was assessed within a convenience sample of 72 community-dwelling individuals with SMI. Semi-structured interviews (n=28) and focus groups (n=4) were subsequently conducted. Results. Within the sample, 45.8% were classified as food insecure, with 29.2% identified as very low food secure. While classic food insecurity barriers (e.g. lack of transportation, fixed income, inadequate resources, etc.) were identified, these factors were further compounded by symptoms associated with mental illness. Conclusions. In comparison to national data, this SMI sample was nearly 8 times more likely to report food insecurity. Information discovered during interviews and focus groups will enable researchers to tailor a food security intervention uniquely suited to address the challenges presented within this population. [Author Abstract]

54.) **Goldberg, S. L.**

Food insecurity among older adults: A social ecological approach.

Ph.D. dissertation, University of Massachusetts, Lowell. 2013.

Food insecurity among U.S. households continues to rise. Food insecurity is defined as "whenever the availability of nutritionally adequate and safe foods, or the ability to acquire adequate foods in socially acceptable ways is limited or uncertain" (Anderson, 1990, p. 1559). Some means of accessing food that may be socially unacceptable including visiting a soup kitchen or food pantry, buying food on credit, relying on friends, family or others for meals, or borrowing money to pay for food (Smith & Richards, 2008). The United States did not reach the Healthy People 2010 goal of reducing household food insecurity by half, to 6%, but rather food insecurity in the US has increased. The US has been in the midst of a profound demographic transition, the rapid aging of its population. Older adults are a group that is vulnerable to health risks. Most older adults have at least one chronic condition and many have more than one or multiple chronic conditions (Administration on Aging [AOA], 2010). There is a need for theory-based research using national samples to better understand food insecurity among this population. Using the social ecological model as the conceptual framework, this study examined the factors that contribute to food insecurity among older adults. This study utilized data from National Health and Nutrition Examination Survey (NHANES) from the years 2007 and 2008 from a sample that included 2,045 adults 60 years of age and older. Multivariate analyses were conducted to determine if the social ecological model helped to explain predictors of food insecurity among older adults. When simultaneously tested in a model, variables emerged as significant from multiple spheres of influence. Analyses of the model indicated that the severity of depression, reports of financial support, and having ever received household food stamp benefits had main effects on food insecurity among older adults that were statistically significant. In addition to the studied hypotheses, marital status, race and ethnicity, education attainment, and private insurance coverage were statistically significant when controlling for all other variables. This study addressed an important health promotion issue and used a social ecological approach to understand factors associated with food insecurity. The study findings have implications for nursing practice, education, and research and could lead to the development of screening methods, interventions, and policy evaluation that focus on food insecurity at multiple spheres of influence. [Author Abstract]

55.) **Goodman, L. G.**

Factors Associated with Food Insecurity among Women in a Small Indigenous Canadian Arctic Community.

M.Sc. thesis, McGill University (Canada). 2009.

Research was conducted to better understand the food insecurity (FI) experience among women in a small indigenous Canadian Arctic community. A descriptive, cross-sectional study was conducted in January-February 2006 with 54 women (20-40 years). Interviews were conducted on food insecurity, lifestyle, health, dietary self-efficacy and traditional food (TF) frequency; anthropometry data were also gathered. FI affected 55% of participating households in the community. Issues of food availability, quality and variety; lack of consumer skills; and lack of TF access were recognized as potential barriers to food security. Women from FI households were more likely to report an inability to access TF (p=0.0171). No associations were found between food security status and dietary self-efficacy or TF frequency of use. Current measures, programs and policies addressing FI need to consider unique barriers facing Indigenous Peoples living in northern Canada, including the barriers that affect access to TF resources. [Author Abstract]

56.) **Harmes, S. A.**

Developing household food insecurity through policies reinforcing dependency on cultivating with chemical agricultural inputs: A case study of Zambia's Chewa.
Ph.D. dissertation, University of Delaware. 2011.

This study investigates the development of food insecurity among the Chewa, a matrilineal agricultural society in the Eastern Province of Zambia. Ethnographic techniques are implemented to obtain information from Respondents volunteering to participate in the study. Prior to colonization the Chewa were considered successful cultivators generally producing a surplus of crops as they maintained a local ecological balance and maintained food security. Unfortunately, Chewa household food security has declined. This study investigates why a successful agricultural society has now become food insecure. Through the various political eras and government policies, the dissertation documents and analyses the conditions which contributed to the increased dependency on chemical agricultural inputs. External influences as determined by the policies promoted by development agencies and international financial institutions are considered in the analysis as well. Keywords: Chewa, Zambia, household food security, chemical input dependence. [Author Abstract]

57.) **Harris, D.**

Household food insecurity and BMI outcomes among pre-school and school aged children in an inner-city setting.

Ph.D. dissertation, Temple University. 2009.

Introduction: While the paradoxical association between overweight and household food insecurity (HFI) is well established amongst low-income women, findings remain inconclusive amongst children. The purpose of this study was to determine the relationship between household food insecurity (HFI) and child overweight outcomes in an inner-city, pre-school and school aged population. Methods: This study used a cross-sectional study design augmented by validated Early Pregnancy Study (EPS) data collected during a pregnancy 6 years prior. A random subset of mothers of child-bearing age (23-44 years) and the child resulting from that pregnancy (between 4-7 years of age at time of re-enrollment) were tracked and re-enrolled in this follow-up study. The primary exposure, HFI, was captured using an adaptation of the standardized US Food Security Scale--embedded within a larger self-report questionnaire addressing selected maternal and child influences (such as health, exercise, and dietary risk factors) on child weight patterns. Maternal and the child BMI outcome was determined through in-home clinical assessment of height and weight and using standard CDC based cutoffs to classify weight status. Self-report and biologically confirmed prenatal EPS data were also obtained to establish useful baseline data and to enhance study results. Exploratory hypotheses examined: (1) Interrelatedness between select maternal and child health, social-environmental, and socio-demographic exposures and (2) Household food insecurity (HFI), prenatal and current maternal and child exposures were explored for their relationship with child BMI. Results: Thirty-six mother-child dyads participated in this follow-up study. Twenty-eight percent of mothers reported HFI; 83% of mothers were classified as overweight or obese and 58% of children were categorized as at-risk for overweight or overweight. Most bi-variate analyses yielded non-significant results, though in-utero drug use was significantly correlated, and mothers who tested positive for tobacco use during pregnancy were also likely to test positive for marijuana use, as determined through biological confirmation ($p<0.05$). Additionally, current maternal BMI as well as current maternal hip-to-waist ratio were each significantly associated with current child BMI ($p<0.05$). One unexpected finding included a significant association between current maternal BMI and presence of a co-morbidity in the child ($p<0.05$). No significant relationships were found between HFI or additional exploratory multivariate models looking at independent effects of prenatal and current maternal-child exposures in predicting child overweight, though current maternal BMI was predictive of child overweight in most analyses. Access to electronic medical record information was highly predictive of participation in this follow-up study ($p<0.001$). Discussion : This study provided an opportunity to better characterize an attrition-prone population, and, while it is possible to track and identify these women through electronic medical record databases, recruitment efforts were labor-intensive and attrition rates particularly high (~22% of mothers re-enrolled). Overall, the influence of household food insecurity on child overweight remains unclear. However, study findings also demonstrated that maternal weight alone was highly predictive of child overweight as early as pre-school, mirroring empirical evidence in this area. Ultimately, childhood obesity is more effectively prevented when treated as a familial concern. Future studies should continue to explore cumulative influences catalyzing obesity in young children in order to better inform understanding of early obesity onset. [Author Abstract]

58.) **Hawley, C. W.**

Broke at the buffet: food insecurity in America.

M.A. thesis, Kansas State University. 2009.

It is the intention of this thesis to come to a better understanding of the factors that lead to food insecurity, a concept for understanding if people have enough food to eat. The tool for household measurement was developed by the United States Department of Agriculture, and is the backbone of the Food Security Supplement, which is conducted annually as part of the Current Population Survey. Three literature are reviewed: concentration of markets, civic agriculture and localism, and food security and nutrition. Each approaches understanding food security from a different angle offering insights along with its shortcomings. Most US studies consider food insecurity as a contributing component of poor health. In this study, I ask instead, "What are the major predictors of household food insecurity?" Using data from the Food Security Supplement of the Current Population Survey from 2000 to 2007, I use descriptive statistics and logistic regression to investigate the causes of food insecurity. I show that as currently measured food insecurity is largely a function of economic inequalities. Within this broad finding, however, I also show that households in a principal city and nonmetropolitan counties are not more likely than other households to experience food insecurity even when controlling for economic and sociodemographic variables. [Author Abstract]

59.) **Hernandez-Garbanzo, Y. M.**

Measuring the impact of youth EFNEP: Questionnaire development and validation. Ph.D. dissertation, Clemson University. 2011.

Background . Given the problem of childhood obesity and food insecurity among low-income children, the Youth Expanded Food and Nutrition Education Program (EFNEP) needs an appropriate, valid and reliable evaluation tool to determine the program effectiveness. Purpose . To describe the development and preliminary validation of EFNEP Youth Quest questionnaire, an impact assessment tool designed for Youth EFNEP program. Use of theory . The Community Nutrition Education logic model adapted with constructs of Social Cognitive Theory and Theory of Planned Behavior. Targeted audience . Low income-ethnically diverse children, in third, fourth and fifth grade. Design . The development of the questionnaire included six phases: preliminary curricula content analysis, conceptualization, construction, expert reviews, cognitive interviews, and revisions. The selected measures were: outcome expectations, self-efficacy, intentions and knowledge related to nutrition, physical activity and food safety. Each measure was assessed with different topics that emerged from a content analysis of multiple Youth EFNEP curricula. Items were selected through the literature review and/or existing instruments; new items were created as necessary. Evaluation . Content validity and face validity were assessed through expert reviews (n=5) and cognitive interviews (n=14), respectively. Data from 452 children was collected for factor analysis, internal consistency and item difficulty analysis. Test-retest reliability was also assessed (n=75). Predictive validity of the nutrition and physical activity scales were assessed using direct measures of food intake (n=62) and physical activity (n=47). Results . Content analysis, expert reviews and cognitive interviews were used to develop the questionnaire and to confirm the content and age appropriateness of the questionnaire. Factor analysis revealed interpretable factors for each of the content domains and served as strategy for item reduction. Item difficulty for knowledge items ranged between 6-92%. Internal consistency for most of the final psychosocial scales was acceptable. Kappa statistics for test-retest reliability ranged between 0.06-0.70. For predictive validity, only 3 out of the 12 hypothesized correlations were significant. Conclusion and implications . Although further work is needed, the preliminary results of this study suggest that EFNEP Youth Quest could be used for evaluating Youth EFNEP programs. This study could serve as framework for designing similar assessment tools for different age groups. [Author Abstract]

60.) **Hilmers, A.**

Associations between household food insecurity, parental self-efficacy and fruit and vegetable parenting practices among parents of 5-8 year old overweight children. M.S. thesis, Texas Woman's University. 2011.

Food insecurity may negatively impact children's dietary intake by affecting parenting quality. This study investigated whether food insecurity influences parental self-efficacy and parenting practices to promote fruit and vegetable consumption. A secondary analysis was conducted using baseline data from 31 mothers of 5-8 year old overweight children who participated in an obesity treatment program. Household food security status, parental self-efficacy (modeling/socialization, planning/encouraging and availability/accessibility) and parenting practices (structure, responsiveness, non-directive control, and external control) were assessed using validated measures. Independent t-tests compared differences by food security status. Results showed no significant differences between food-secure and insecure groups. A trend towards a decrease in parental self-efficacy to make fruit and vegetables available and accessible at home was observed in the food-insecure group. This finding supports further hypothesis-driven research examining the impact of food insecurity on parental self-efficacy and food-related parenting practices. [Author Abstract]

61.) **Hinds, H. E.**

The relationships between food insecurity and iron, folate and vitamin B(12) status in the elderly.

Ph.D. dissertation, Howard University. 2006.

Although millions of elderly individuals in the United States (US) and internationally are affected by food insecurity, limited information is available on its effects on nutritional status. Hence, data from the National Health and Nutrition Examination Survey 2001--2002 were utilized to examine the relationships of food insecurity to socio-demographic variables, gender, and iron, folate, and vitamin B 12 status in the elderly ≥ 60 years old. Statistical analyses (t-tests, chi square tests, and multiple logistic regression) were performed using the SUDAAN software package. Dietary intakes and biochemical values of iron, folate, and vitamin B12 status; socio-demographic data, gender, and body mass index (BMI) were analyzed. Of the 1770 subjects, 1,540 (87%) were food secure and 230 (13%) were food insecure. Limited education, low income (≤$14,999), being single or never married, and Black or Mexican American ethnicity were significantly related to food insecurity. Food insecure subjects and females had significantly lower dietary intakes than food secure and male subjects respectively. Whites and subjects with higher income levels tended to have significantly higher dietary intakes than minorities and lower income persons. Food insecure subjects had significantly lower serum iron, red blood cell (RBC) and serum folate levels than food secure subjects. Females in comparison to males had significantly lower biochemical measures of iron status, folate, vitamin B 12 , and hemoglobin levels. Whites tended to have significantly higher biochemical measures of folate status than other ethnic groups, while Blacks and Mexican Americans had significantly higher vitamin B12 levels, and other Hispanics had the highest iron values. White females showed higher blood concentrations of TIBC and folate levels than minority women. Mexican American women had higher levels of iron, transferrin saturation, and vitamin B12 compared with women of other ethnic groups. groups. Other Hispanics had higher ferritin levels; whereas, Blacks had low values of hemoglobin, folate, and iron. Higher income levels were generally associated with greater biochemical measures of iron, folate, and vitamin B 12 status. Multiple logistic regression analysis indicated significant relationships between food security and food /olute (OR = 1.02, 1.00, 1.04), serum iron (OR = 0.97, 0.93, 1.00), and RBC folate (OR = 0.99, 0.98, 1.00). Further studies are needed to address the relationships of food security to nutritional, emotional, social, and psychological problems in the elderly. [Author Abstract]

62.) **Hoffman, K.**

Food insecurity and Oregon TANF leavers.

Ph.D. dissertation, Portland State University. 2007.

Food security, as defined in the U.S., means access by all people at all times to enough food for an active, healthy life. Examining the risk factors and consequences of food insecurity for those who leave Temporary Assistance for Needy Families (TANF) has practical implications, but empirical research has lagged behind theory. This study tested the Campbell Model of Food Insecurity (1991), a previously untested theoretical model, in a sample of TANF leavers in Oregon (n=637 Wave 1, n=552 Wave 2). Additionally, a qualitative examination of Oregon Food Bank workers, Oregon's largest charitable emergency food organization, was conducted to gather insight about how food insecurity is affecting their organization and their clients. Results of the structural equation modeling analyses addressing three risk items (financial hardship, income and education) and three health items (physical health, mental health and activities of daily living) suggested that (a) higher levels of financial hardship and lower levels of income and education led to poorer physical health, mental health, and diminished activities of daily living due to health; (b) higher levels of financial hardship---but not income or education---led to food insecurity; (c) higher levels of food insecurity led to poorer physical health, mental health, and diminished activities of daily living due to health; and (d) food insecurity did not mediate the relationships between the three risk items and the three health items with one exception: in the cross-sectional model of Wave 2 data, food insecurity mediated the relationship between financial hardship and all three health outcomes. Themes that emerged from the exploratory and descriptive case study of Oregon Food Bank personnel echo these results. Interviews were analyzed using content analysis and seven themes emerged as important facets or concerns for their work. Respondents universally agreed that food insecurity was adversely affecting the health of their clients and reported ways in which they are attempting to ameliorate these connections. Respondents also reported on conflicts they have encountered in trying to address the agency's two aims: feeding the hungry and addressing the root causes of hunger. [Author Abstract]

63.) **Howard, L. L.**

Essays on public economics and health in the U.S.

Ph.D. dissertation, University of Houston. 2008.

Quantifying the benefits and determining factors of government expenditure on public welfare programs is of policy concern. In this dissertation, I present two essays that empirically investigate two large scale public programs currently implemented in the U.S. Overall, the results provide important cautionary tales for policymakers contemplating changes in the scope of public welfare programs. First, I model the effects of subsidizing school lunch on the noncognitive performance of children with food insecurity at home. I estimate static simultaneous equation models for children's noncognitive performance at school using longitudinal data on 4,282 students in the USA enrolled in 1st, 3rd, and 5th grade (1999-2003) of the Early Childhood Longitudinal Study-Kindergarten. Results indicate that household food insecurity is significantly ($P<0.05$) negatively associated with measures of noncognitive skill; however, contemporaneous participation in the National School Lunch Program mitigates the deleterious effect. Further findings underscore the vital influence that parental education has in determining the weekly food consumption patterns of young children and their subsequent weight gain. Second, I construct and utilize a panel of U.S. states over 20 years to examine state government demand for the provision of low income public health care through the Medicaid program. Reallocation of expenditure within the program and between other welfare expenditure is modeled using the demand system developed in Deaton and Muellbauer (1980). I disaggregate the recipient population of Medicaid into distinct demographic groups consisting of the elderly, the disabled, and families, and estimate inter-group substitution patterns between the recipient and benefit dimensions of programmatic design. The main findings are, first, states work to finance the costs of eligibility or benefit changes in part through alterations of existing health care provisions. Second, states respond unequally to program cost increases affecting each of the groups and disproportionately reduce expenditure on the disabled. Third, the partisan composition of state governments significantly affects Medicaid spending decisions. Republican regimes are pro-elderly and pro-families, while Democrat regimes are pro-disabled. [Author Abstract]

64.) **Hromi-Fiedler, A.**

Nutrient intakes, food insecurity, pregnancy weight gain and birth outcomes among Connecticut Latinas.

Ph.D. dissertation, University of Connecticut. 2007.

The primary objectives of this prospective study were to: (1) adapt and validate the U.S. Household Food Security Scale among pregnant Latinas; (2) describe nutrient intake patterns among Latina subgroups; and (3) document household food insecurity before as well as during pregnancy and examine it's influence on pregnancy weight gain and infant birth weight among pregnant Latina women living in Hartford, Connecticut. Both qualitative and quantitative methods were used to fulfill these objectives. Focus groups were conducted among pregnant Latina women to adapt the U.S. Household Food Security Scale (FSS). Data from 241 participants who participated in the prenatal baseline survey for this study was used to assess the psychometric performance of the FSS. The final adapted version of the FSS was used to assess household food insecurity before and during pregnancy. Dietary intake and meal skipping patterns during pregnancy were assessed via a 24-hour recall and meal skipping questionnaire. Pregnancy and infant outcomes were obtained at a postpartum visit as well as through medical records. Univariate and bivariate analyses were used to evaluate the relationship between (1) nutrient intakes and ethnicity and (2) household food security (independent variables) and dependent variables (gestational weight gain and birthweight). Multivariate logistic regression analyses was used to assess the associations between (1) ethnicity, frequency of fast food restaurant use, and nutrient intakes, and (2) household food insecurity, gestational weight gain and infant birthweight. The results from this study indicate that (1) the adapted household food security scale is valid for the target population, (2) nutrient intake patterns vary between Puerto Rican and non-Puerto Rican Latinas, and (3) household food security status is associated with gestational weight gain and low birth weight. Findings have important implications for food security policies and nutrition education, as well as monitoring risk of adverse pregnancy and birth outcomes among Latinas. [Author Abstract]

65.) **Huet, C.**

Prevalence and correlates of food insecurity in Inuit communities.

M.Sc. thesis, McGill University (Canada). 2011.

Limited information is available on food security prevalence in Inuit populations. The majority of research is limited to a small number of communities. Under the International Polar Year, a cross-sectional Inuit Health Survey was conducted which included 2595 adults from 36 Inuit communities. Information on community, household, individual and dietary characteristics was collected throughout interviews and clinical assessments. Food security status of households and adults was measured using the USDA food security survey module. Overall, 33.6% of households were moderately food insecure and 29.1% were severely food insecure. Household crowding, low education and income, Healthy Eating Index scores ($P \leq 0.001$) and other dietary characteristics were associated with increased risk of food insecurity. [Author Abstract]

66.) **Ichimi, G. S.**

The World Trade Organisation and food insecurity in the south: prospects for the ECOWAS sub-region.

Ph.D. dissertation, University of Aberdeen (Australia). 2013.

This thesis focuses on the topic 'The World Trade Organisation and Food Insecurity in the South: Prospects for the ECOWAS sub-region'. It is cast against the background of the prevailing global food crisis which is generally accepted as having assumed monumental dimensions in sub-Saharan Africa where a total of over 150 million people are said to be under the direct threat of hunger and starvation. The study appraises the mainstream understanding of the root causes of the on-going food crisis, the policies prescribed for their resolution as well as the efficacy of the neo-liberal multilateral institutional frameworks from within which these are currently being deployed. The global and regional multilateral institutions of reference here are the World Trade Organisation (WTO) and the Economic Community of West African States (ECOWAS) respectively. The study contends that the hegemonic narrative is severely limited; that the perspective which drives it suffers from some highly virulent blind-spots on the critical questions of history and the structural notions of power – notions which go to the very heart of the contemporary structuring of the global food system, and which, in the case of West Africa, is assuring the privileged access of some classes to food and food-producing resources whilst excluding the bulk of the class of the majority. Consequently, from a macro-historical qualitative perspective, the study develops and deploys an alternative conceptual framework from within which it appraises the regional agricultural and related trade policies of the member states of the ECOWAS which were developed in response to the neoliberal regimes of the WTO. With the reality of third world structural dependency as a point of departure, and situating this within the theoretical framework of Robert W. Cox and the tenets of Dependency theory, the study poses the question of whether and/or how, in the specific instance of West Africa, the framing of the region's food and agricultural policies, couched as they have been in conformity to the broader context of the regimes of the WTO, has resulted in the aggravation of insecurity in food production and consumption. Pursuant to investigating this question, the study finds that as adherence by the member states of the ECOWAS to the rules of the WTO Agreements in particular and the dictates of neoliberal economic agenda in general intensifies, regional food and agricultural development strategies of the region have invariably proven incapable of overcoming the logic of structural capitalist dependency. Rather, as the ECOWAP achieves coincidence with the regimes of the WTO, those exact material conditions that stymie the prospects for structural transformation of the agrarian economy in the West African sub-region are being reinforced. The exacerbation of the associated problems of agricultural productivity decline, as well as the concomitant loss of household and national incomes is effectively putting even the food that is available both in the local and international markets well beyond the reach of the bulk of the poverty stricken majority of the people of Western Africa. [Author Abstract]

67.) **Jalal, C. S. B.**

Effects of BRAC's poverty reduction program targeting the ultra-poor in rural Bangladesh.

Ph.D. dissertation, Cornell University. 2008.

Poverty alleviation programs for the extreme poor improve participants' economic status and may also impact other important outcomes that are seldom evaluated. Challenging the Frontiers of Poverty Reduction/Targeting the Ultra Poor (CFPR/TUP), a program implemented by Building Resources Across Communities (BRAC), has been successful in significantly alleviating extreme poverty in rural Bangladesh. We hypothesized that the program also improved participants' subjective wellbeing and nutritional status (i.e., weight-for-height) of children, and decreased food insecurity, domestic violence, and distress. A non-equivalent pre- and post-test quasi-experimental design was used to test the hypotheses. Data were collected from a random sample of 1618 (640 program and 978 control) households across 261 villages under 38 BRAC Area Offices of 3 northern districts of Bangladesh in 2002 and 2005-2006. Linear mixed random-intercept models were used to control for the clustering effects and other potential confounders. Program households in 2006 were significantly better than the control households in women's subjective wellbeing ($p<0.001$) and weight-for-height of children between ages 24-35 months ($p<0.01$), and lower in food insecurity ($p<0.001$) and domestic violence ($p<0.01$). Reduced food insecurity was a substantial mediator of program effects on other outcomes. The results of this study are highly important as this is a large-scale program already extended to half of the country. Findings will contribute in judging the cost-benefit and cost-effectiveness of the program, and in garnering support for the expansion of such programs. [Author Abstract]

68.) **Jang, S. Y.**

Associations of food insecurity, socioeconomic status, and type 2 diabetes among Mexican Americans and non-Hispanic whites in the United States.

M.S. thesis, Rutgers University. 2009.

Mexican Americans are the largest segment of Hispanics in the United States of America (U.S.). Hispanics and Mexican Americans are more likely to have higher rates of type 2 diabetes (T2D) and its risk factors such as obesity, physical inactivity, low socioeconomic status (SES), and food insecurity compared to non-Hispanic Whites (NHW). However, the research looking into the associations between these risk factors and T2D, and the potential racial/ethnic differences is limited. This study examined whether food insecurity was related to T2D independently of low SES and a wide range of T2D risk factors among Mexican Americans and non-Hispanic Whites (NHW) in a nationally representative sample in the U.S. About 12,944 adults, including 2,955 Mexican Americans and 6,363 non-Hispanic Whites, 20-84yr, from the National Health and Nutrition Examination Survey (NHANES) 1999-2004 were included in the analyses. Multivariate logistic regression analyses indicated that participants with marginal or very low food security (vs. high food security) at the household level were more likely to have T2D after adjusting for education, employment, poverty, race/ethnicity, age, gender, and country of birth ($p<0.05$). Following further adjustment for obesity, lifestyle factors (physical activity, cigarette smoking, alcohol and dietary intakes), family history of diabetes, and comorbidities, participants with very low (household) food security remained more likely to have T2D (OR 1.84, CI 1.02-3.31). When the two racial/ethnic groups were examined separately, very low food security became a stronger determinant of T2D among NHWs (OR 3.53, CI 1.58-7.87), but this association was attenuated among Mexican Americans. Low SES, as determined by education and employment levels, were marginally related to higher likelihood of having T2D among Mexican Americans (p=0.050) but not among NHWs. These results suggest that associations of food insecurity and SES with T2D vary between Mexican American and NHW adults. This may require different approaches for prevention efforts tailored to the needs of each racial/ethnic group. [Author Abstract]

69.) **Jemal, A.**

The deadly crossroads: The role of household food insecurity and nutritional status in antiretroviral therapy (ART) outcomes; HIV+ adult treatment failure as an important public health challenge in sub-Saharan Africa, Ethiopia.

M.P.H. thesis, Yale University. 2009.

Background: Currently, the antiretroviral therapy (ART) programs in sub-Saharan Africa do not integrate nutrition as part of their ART management. In Ethiopia, HIV positive patients face significant challenges in terms of accessing basic nutrition. Objective: This study focuses on elucidating the role of nutrition and household food insecurity on HIV drug adherence outcomes. Methods: Body Mass Index (BMI), Mid-Upper Arm Circumference (MUAC), and Hemoglobin (Hg) were used to assess nutritional status over time. Household Food Insecurity Access scale (HFIAS) was used to categorize patients according to level of food insecurity. Adherence data was collected using the AIDS Clinical Trial Group (ACTG) questionnaire, CD4 T cell counts and total lymphocytes were obtained from patient chart. Bivariate analyses of anthropometric and food insecurity indicators were used to examine the determinants of ART non-adherence. Multivariate logistic regression was also used to examine the net effect of each independent variable in the model on nutrition and food insecurity. Results: Of 60 patients, 50 (83.3%) reported ≤95% level of ART adherence. Women are slightly higher (55%) of the HIV study group. Anemia is more prevalent among women (43%) compared with men (32%) at the start of ART. Bivariate analysis shows that BMI categories at 6 month and 2 years are significantly associated with ART-non adherence. BMI categories at 2 years period show that non-adherence is 27% among underweight, 9% among normal and 50% among overweight categories. Adjusted multivariate logistic regression shows that normal weight category at 2 years is significantly associated with ART nonadherence. MUAC categories show that 60% of the HIV patient population at Chiro is malnourished. HFIAS score also shows that 92% of the HIV positive patients are severely food insecure while 8% are moderately food insecure. Common clinical symptoms thought to be associated with nutrition include wasting (47%), fever (43%) and diarrhea (32%). Conclusion: While self-reported adherence among the sample from Chiro hospital is relatively high, food insecurity remains a major challenge. The impact of mandating nutrition as part of the ART program needs further examination. [Author Abstract]

70.) **Johnson, H. E.**

Reproduction, exchange relations and food insecurity: maize production and maize markets in Honduras.

Ph.D. dissertation, Open University (United Kingdom). 1995.

Although severe poverty and difficult climatic conditions for crop production created acute food insecurity among many small maize producers in parts of Honduras in the 1980s, this thesis focuses on the widespread phenomenon of chronic and endemic vulnerability found in less critically affected parts of the country. It argues that a major cause of food insecurity among small maize producers in the 1980s lay in the complex nature of social relations of production and exchange for maize. Nevertheless, policy debates and directions in Honduras tended to side-step these complexities. A key distinction between maize production and trade was that the latter was driven by profits while the former continued in production even though many farmers had negative net cash incomes. Traders' profits also depended on social differentiation, by wealth and task in trade, as on the differentiation of farmers from whom they purchased maize. Personalised relations also helped to ensure profits from trade. Although maize trade involved many participants and was apparently competitive, local traders (including commercial maize farmers) could establish debt relations with semi-proletarian farmers which put the latter at a disadvantage in output markets, especially with respect to the time of maize sales and hence prices received. Market alternatives for semi-proletarian farmers were relatively restricted compared to commercial farmers and petty commodity producers. The thesis concludes that policies which only consider market variables in maize production and distribution and which propose increasing liberalisation and deregulation are unlikely to benefit those who are most at risk among Honduran maize farmers. Unless the complex social relations which maintain either the stagnation of semi-proletarian farmers or the insecure transformation of petty commodity producers are addressed, conditions of reproducing maize production are likely to become more acute and reinforce food insecurity in the countryside. [Author Abstract]

71.) **Jorosi-Tshiamo, W. B.**

Dietary intake of children aged 1 year to 5 years and their anthropometric measures in Kweneng district-Botswana.

Ph.D. dissertation, Case Western Reserve University. 2012.

Background: The nutritional well-being of young children is positively and negatively affected by the interaction between food intake, health and care. Most important, inadequate intake of food, energy and nutrients remains highly prevalent in developing countries. Dietary standards designed to provide guidelines on basic nutrients for sufficient growth and health that are found in the developed countries do not exist or are not accessible to many in the third world or developing countries. Purpose: The major focus of this study was to describe and explore the relationship between the food and beverages consumed by children aged 1 to 5 years and their anthropometric measurements as well as to determine the relationships between the children's food and beverage consumption, caregiver's household food security and children's anthropometric measures. Methods: A cross-sectional descriptive - correlational design was used. A convenience sample including 99 pairs of caregivers and their children was recruited from six clinical sites. Data collection employed face-to-face interviews and the participants responded to three instruments. The instruments included the Caregiver Demographic Data Form, Child Food Frequency Questionnaire and the Household Food Security Scale. In addition, anthropomorphic measurement including heights and weights were obtained from children. Data were analyzed by descriptive methods, the Pearson product moment correlations, independent sample t-tests and one-way ANOVA. Results: The caregivers were aged 18 to 65 years (M = 33.65, SD = 10.50) and children's ages ranged from12-56 months (M = 28.99, SD = 12.9). Five percent had weight-for-height z-scores at -1, while 16.2% had HAZ that were below the -2 z-score indicating stunted growth. Thirty-one percent of children were at risk for overweight. The five core/main food items that were frequently consumed by the children were sorghum, milk, sugar, tea/coffee and yoghurt. The mean energy intake was 1618.4 kcal/d, (SD = 713.4) and the mean protein intake was 45.9 g/d (SD = 22.1). Nineteen percent of caregivers were food secure while 28.3% and 20.2% were moderately and severely food insecure respectively. The independent samples t-test revealed statistically significant differences among the household food security score means for caregivers with low and high education, suggesting that caregivers with low education were more likely to be food insecure than their counterparts with higher education. Children's total energy and protein intakes were statistically significant and moderately correlated with height and weight (r (97) =.35 p<.01 and r (97) =.32 p<.01) 2-tailed). The one-way ANOVA results were [F (2, 96) = 9.19, p<.05] (energy) and [F (2, 96) = 6.59, p<.05] (protein). These findings indicated that the average intake of energy and protein differed according to the age groups of children. Conclusion: Overall, the findings show that children in the study consumed a limited number of food items that may lead to inadequate intake of nutrients such as vitamins and minerals. In addition, the prevalence of household food insecurity, stunting of growth among children and the BMI suggestive of higher risk for overweight warrant further investigation. Future longitudinal studies should examine the associations between dietary patterns and child health and development to provide evidence needed to improve dietary advice given to parents of young children. [Author Abstract]

72.) **Jung, S. E.**

Comparison of factors influencing body weight among diverse individuals receiving food stamps.

M.S. thesis, Oklahoma State University. 2008.

Scope and Method of Study:. The purpose of this study was to obtain a greater understanding of factors influencing body weight among diverse racial/ethnic groups receiving Food Stamps. A Random Digit Dial survey was administered to a representative sample of individuals 30-44 years of age who received food stamp benefits from November 2005 to January 2006. Data was obtained from 100 individuals from each racial/ethnic group, namely White, African American, Native American and Hispanic, in the state of Oklahoma. Descriptive statistics were used to summarize demographic data such as age, marriage status, education level, ethnicity, employment, monthly income, and BMI. ANOVA procedures were used to test the null hypothesis that there were no significant differences in means of body satisfaction scores, body image behavior scores, food security scores, and BMI among different racial groups. Findings and Conclusions: It has been reported that differences in obesity are associated with a significant difference in perception of body image among diverse ethnic groups and that these differences in perceptions of body image affect weight change and weight control. Results from our study indicate few differences when data was analyzed using race as the independent variable. However, more significant differences were found when the data was analyzed using food security status as the independent variable. We posit that ethnic differences are not as evident when individuals share common experiences such as poverty and body weight status. It is possible that being in poverty is a more influential factor on body weight than ethnicity among individuals of limited resources. [Author Abstract]

73.) **Jyoti, D. F.**

Modifying effects of participation in federal child nutrition programs on the developmental consequences of household food insecurity for children.

Ph.D. dissertation, Cornell University. 2006.

Food insecurity remains a persistent public health problem for children in the U.S. and is thought to have consequences for child physical, social and academic development. The School Breakfast Program, the National School Lunch Program, and Supplemental Food and Nutrition Program for Women, Infants and Children (WIC) are federally funded programs intended to avert food insecurity and its consequences for children. These nutrition programs have also been associated with child physical, social and academic developmental outcomes. Further research is needed to investigate the complex relations between variables and to establish greater plausibility that associations are causal in nature. This study investigated the causal effects of household food insecurity and child nutrition program participation by using longitudinal data and statistical methods to account for potential bias. Fixed-effects modeling was utilized to minimize bias resulting from selection to participate and to take advantage of dynamic changes in household food insecurity status and program participation between kindergarten and 3rd grade. Household food insecurity, independent of household income and other child- and household-level factors, was associated with poorer social skills and reading performance development among girls, and with greater weight gain among boys. National School Lunch Program participation was associated with better mathematics and reading performance for children. The effects of National School Lunch Program participation were stronger for children with greater socioeconomic need compared to those with less socioeconomic need, suggesting that food assistance participation may impact child development by modifying the effects of stress-related hardships. Neither school breakfast participation nor school lunch participation was associated with greater weight gain. In conclusion, food insecurity may exert its detrimental effects through nutritional and non-nutritional (i.e., stress-related) mechanisms. Similarly, school nutrition programs may protect children against the effects of food insecurity through nutritional and non-nutritional mechanisms. Further research into potential mechanisms underlying these associations is warranted. Policy implications of the findings are discussed. [Author Abstract]

74.) **Kaba, K. D.**

Determinants of household food insecurity and associated coping strategies in 2 health zones of Kinshasa, Democratic Republic of Congo, during and after 1996--2002 war periods.

Ph.D. dissertation, Tulane University. 2009.

From 1996 to 2002, the Democratic Republic of Congo (DRC) experienced numerous outbreaks of war. Kinshasa, the Capital, was isolated from its main sources of local food supply which led to a sharp deterioration of the life quality. In 2003, with the Sun City Accord signed formally ending the protracted war, the political and economic situation of the country seemed better. Yet, the household food situation did not seem to improve. This study aimed to increase the general understanding of food insecurity at the household level. The objectives were to determine households' food-insecure based on household socioeconomic and demographic characteristics, to identify coping strategies used by households to manage the food crisis, and to assess differences between the two time periods. A total of 1,591 households from two selected health zones of Kinshasa were surveyed in 2001 and 2004 using a multiple stage-cluster design. A 16-question measure was developed using a summative scale to capture the food security status. Two binary logistic regressions were run to predict food insecurity and identify coping strategies. Interactions were tested in the models to assess differences between the two time periods. Comparisons of proportions and odds ratio were also computed. Households whose chief had none, primary or secondary levels of education, and households with little crafts or jobs as main source of incomes were food-insecure. Change of meal composition, food aid from nutritional centers, and reduction of persons in charge were the main coping strategies used by households food-insecure. No interaction tested in the two models was significant. Households were more likely to be food-insecure during the war period, and the prevalence of determinants and that of coping strategies were also higher during the war period. These research findings provided a better and in-depth understanding of household food insecurity regarding determinants and coping strategies. The relationships between determinants as well as coping strategies and food insecurity were consistent across time, although the observed differences between the two contexts. Political and economic stability of the country should be ensured, salaries paid regularly, post primary education promoted, and food program interventions implemented for sustainable development. [Author Abstract]

75.) **Kasie, T.**

Vulnerability to food insecurity in three agro-ecological zones in Sayint District, Ethiopia.

M.S. thesis, University of Cape Town (South Africa). 2009.

Includes bibliographical references (leaves 113-119). The objective of this study was to identify and compare the determinants of vulnerability to food insecurity among households in three different agro-ecological zones within the rural district of Sayint in South Wollo, Ethiopia. It also sought to apply the livelihoods framework and examine its robustness in this research context. Findings and analysis indicate that oxen ownership, livestock ownership and access to off-farm employment opportunities are the most significant determinants of a households vulnerability to food insecurity. All of the sampled households reported major agricultural problems, such as lack of adequate land, financial constraints and lack of oxen and farm implements, but highland households were found to be more vulnerable to food insecurity than lowland and midland households were. Food security analysis also indicated that 80% of highland households were found to be food insecure. The depth (60%) and severity (41%) of food insecurity were specifically found to be higher among highland households than among lowland and midland households. More detailed vulnerability and livelihood analysis suggest that food insecurity in the highland households is specifically attributed to their limited internal resources endowments and lower access to external assistance.; Includes abstract. [Author Abstract]

76.) **Kent, B. D.**

Food Insecurity as a Factor in Felonious or Misdemeanor Juvenile Crimes.

Ph.D. dissertation, Walden University. 2013.

The sociology of food theory details how access to food may influence social skills and behaviors. As an increasing number of juveniles are incarcerated in public and private detaining centers, the question arises of whether the problem may stem from food insecure homes. Determining whether a food insecure household is a factor in juvenile delinquency may aid in the rehabilitation process for this population. In this study, a quantitative analysis was conducted to determine if a difference existed between food insecurity and the number of felony crimes (N = 290) committed versus the number of misdemeanor crimes (N = 294) committed by juvenile delinquents (N = 584) in 7 U.S. States. A comparison was made between the juveniles' food security and the crime they committed. Food security was determined using the juveniles' height and weight to calculate their body mass index (kg/m 2). Statistical analysis included a z score to compare the crime types, and a 2-tailed t test to determine the significance of the population. There was no significant difference in the food security of those who committed a felony (M = 23.83, SD = 3.98) and those who committed a misdemeanor (M = 23.72, SD = 3.57, p = 0.73). Food secure juveniles who committed misdemeanors comprised 97.96% of the population, whereas food secure juveniles who committed felonies accounted for 97.58% of the population. In turn, food insecure juveniles who committed misdemeanors comprised 2.41%, whereas food insecure juveniles who committed felonies accounted for 2.04% of the population. These findings suggest that all crimes are being committed by juveniles. The issue of juvenile delinquency should remain in the forefront of those tasked to promote rehabilitation, such as detention center administrators, to ensure this negative behavior does not follow the juvenile into adulthood. [Author Abstract]

77.) **Kepple, A. W.**

County-level policy-making related to hunger and food insecurity: The role of information and ideology.

Ph.D. dissertation, Cornell University. 1997.

This interpretive study examined influences on hunger-related policy making at the county level with a focus on the role of information and ideology. The research questions focused on three concerns: decision makers' conceptualizations of hunger; face validity of existing measures of hunger; and influences on hunger-related decisions. Open-ended interviews were conducted with thirty-two decision makers in three rural counties and eight state-level decision makers in New York State. Fifteen meetings were observed and documents reviewed. One county was the primary focus of the study because of a hunger survey conducted there. Most decision makers attributed hunger to a combination of two causes: (1) economic factors that are systemic (not self-induced); and (2) inefficient household budgeting (self-induced). Their perceived solutions to hunger were constrained by their beliefs about the causes of hunger and the limits of government. Predominant beliefs that hunger is largely self-induced and that government's role should be limited operated to suppress hunger from the agenda at the local level. Decision makers' conceptualizations of hunger and food insecurity matched the conceptualization that has emerged from hunger research. Both conceptualize hunger as a process progressing from (1) anxiety about food supply and compromised diet quality (food insecurity), to (2) inadequate quantity of food for adults (hunger), to (3) inadequate quantity of food for children (the most severe hunger). Existing measures of hunger had face validity for many decision makers. However, the more a decision maker believed that hunger is self-induced, the less inclined they were to believe measures of hunger are valid. The most effective type of information depended on decision makers' beliefs about causes and solutions for hunger; where hunger was on decision makers' agenda; and the nature of the decision. Strong beliefs that hunger is self induced and government intervention should be limited, and higher position of the issue on the policy agenda, required more convincing information. Descriptive data can be effectively targeted to routine program decisions about funding and resource allocation. More conceptual research may influence decision makers' thinking over time for broader policy decisions characterized by more diffuse decision making processes. [Author Abstract]

78.) **Khachadourian, I. R.**

The prevalence of food insecurity among reentry women students and their children at California State University, Fresno.

M.P.H. thesis, California State University, Fresno. 1999.

The purpose of this study was to examine the prevalence of food insecurity among the reentry women students and their children at California State University, Fresno. The effect of food insecurity on their academic performance and ways in which the Reentry Program can support women who wish to make the transition from welfare recipient to reentry student were also examined. A questionnaire was distributed to a convenience sample of 100 women; 49 women responded. Counts, measures of central tendencies and percentages were compiled. The effect of food insecurity on GPA was analyzed by calculations of chi square statistics. Forty-three percent of reentry women were classified as food insecure, which is significantly higher than the 11.9% national average. Chi square calculations proved that food insecurity has a significant effect on students' GPA. Findings and recommendations were presented for personal, community, institutional, and public domain. [Author Abstract]

79.) **Kim, K.**

Impact of food insecurity and food assistance programs on nutrition and health outcomes in elders.

Ph.D. dissertation, Cornell University. 2005.

This research examined the relationship between need and help-seeking behavior over time in elders, looking at the pattern of food insecurity and program participation, which are a part of need and help-seeking behavior. Then, it assessed how a help-seeking behavior (i.e., participation in food assistance programs) among elders in need (i.e., food insecure elders) affected multiple outcomes such as obesity, depression, and health service utilization. For addressing these research questions, secondary data analysis was done using two longitudinal data sets: Health and Retirement Study (HRS, 1996-2002) and the Asset and Health Dynamics Among the Oldest Old (AHEAD, 1995-2002). The finding on patterns of food insecurity and participation in food assistance programs over time showed that need and help-seeking behavior were changeable but the variation over time was small. The relationship between them was monotonic and increasing. Food insecurity was a useful indicator of need for participation in food assistance programs and previous experience of participation was an important indicator of help-seeking behavior. While food insecurity was a part of need for participation in food assistance programs, for health service utilization it appeared to be a barrier that makes food insecure elders be less likely to use health services. While food insecurity increased overweight and depression, participation in food assistance programs had beneficial impacts on poor health outcomes resulting from food insecurity. Food insecure elders who participated in food assistance programs were less overweight, depressed, and admitted to hospital and nursing home than those who did not participate in the programs. Findings of positive impacts on reducing or preventing obesity, depression, and admission to hospital and nursing home implies other benefits of food assistance programs such as decreased health-care expenditures and increased independence of elders, supporting further development of these programs for elders. [Author Abstract]

80.) **Kirkpatrick, S.**

Household food insecurity in Canada: An examination of nutrition implications and factors associated with vulnerability.

Ph.D. dissertation, University of Toronto (Canada). 2008.

Household food insecurity, defined as "the inability to acquire or consume an adequate diet quality or sufficient quantity of food in socially acceptable ways, or the uncertainty that one will be able to do so," affected almost one in ten Canadian households in 2004. Responses have been dominated by community-based food initiatives with little attention paid to potential policy directions to alleviate this problem. The lack of impetus for policy responses may stem from the paucity of evidence documenting the nutrition implications of household food insecurity. Further, the development of policy interventions is hindered by a lack of understanding of the factors that influence vulnerability to food insecurity. This thesis comprises three studies aimed at providing stimulus and directions for policy responses to household food insecurity in Canada. The first study, an analysis of data from the 2004 Canadian Community Health Survey, documents poorer dietary intakes and heightened risk of nutrient inadequacies among adults and adolescents in food-insecure households, providing evidence of the public health implications and public policy relevance of household food insecurity. The second and third studies are examinations of household-level factors associated with vulnerability to household food insecurity. Analysis of data from the 2001 Survey of Household Spending demonstrates the relevance of housing costs to household food access. Among lower-income households, as the proportion of income allocated to housing costs increased, the adequacy of household food spending declined significantly. Receipt of a housing subsidy was associated with an improvement in food spending but mean food spending adequacy fell below the cost of a basic nutritious diet even among subsidized households. The final study comprises a cross-sectional survey of 464 low-income Toronto families, two-thirds of whom were food insecure over the preceding 12 months. Analysis of predictors of severe food insecurity highlights the centrality of income and housing costs and raises serious questions about current definitions of housing affordability and the adequacy of current housing subsidy levels. This work provides a public health imperative for action and points to the urgent need for social policy reform to ameliorate problems of household food insecurity in Canada. [Author Abstract]

81.) **Kuku, O.**

Three essays on food insecurity and child welfare.

Ph.D. dissertation, Iowa State University. 2009.

Three major issues affecting the welfare of children are investigated in three papers in this dissertation. These issues are the intra-household allocation of resources, food insecurity and obesity. The first two papers are focused on the issue of intra-household allocation of food resources and food insecurity in a developing country setting, namely Zimbabwe, while the relationship between food insecurity and obesity is investigated n the United States. In the first paper, a 2004 household survey of children in Zimbabwe is utilized to investigate differences in self-reports of food insecurity. A bivariate ordered probit regression is utilized to investigate any differences in reports of food insecurity between boys and girls. Findings reveal that all categories of children report roughly the same level of food security with the exception of orphan girls, who are significantly more likely to report food insecurity. The second paper is also focused on the intra-household allocation of food, this time between adults and children. Bivariate comparisons are utilized to highlight the magnitude of differences in the perception of food inadequacy and food insecurity, while bivariate probit regressions provide more insight into sources of these differences. Children are more likely than adults to report food security, although the differences are not uniform across households. A substantial number of households have children who are food inadequate or food insecure while the adult is not. In addition, there is evidence of a tendency to protect younger children and discriminate against female orphans in food distribution. The third paper utilizes nonparametric approaches and two nationally representative data sets to investigate the relationship between food insecurity and obesity in the United States. Nonparametric approaches are utilized to portray possible subtleties in the relationship between food insecurity and obesity over the full range of body mass index (BMI)-based percentiles of children in different racial and socioeconomic categories. The relationship between food insecurity and childhood obesity is revealed to be nonlinear and complex. More specifically, there is a strong positive association between food insecurity and age-gender based BMI percentiles for children who are low food secure or very low food secure. This positive association is consistent across a range of racial and socio-economic subgroups, and also across both data sets. [Author Abstract]

82.) **LaCour, M.**

The prevalence of food insecurity and associated factors among households with children in Head Start programs in Houston, Texas and Birmingham, Alabama.

M.P.H. thesis, The University of Texas School of Public Health. 2007.

The purposes of this study were to determine the prevalence of food insecurity and factors associated with food insecurity among households with children enrolled in Head Start programs in Houston, Texas, and Birmingham, Alabama. This cross-sectional study utilized data gathered from 688 households recruited by convenience sample from two Head Start districts in each city. Interviewers collected data from primary caregivers on demographic characteristics, dietary intake, and the six-item USDA food security module. Chi-square and logistic regression analysis were used to determine the association of food security and demographic characteristics. Comparison of means was used to analyze the association between the child's fruit and vegetable intake and the household's food security status. The prevalence of food insecurity among the sample was 34.9% (95% CI: 31.3%, 38.5%). Characteristics associated with food insecurity were the caregiver's national origin (Foreign-born (ref.) v. U.S.-born, adjusted OR = 0.36, 95% CI: 0.14, 0.94), gender of the child (male (ref.) v. female, adjusted OR = 1.44, 95% CI: 1.03, 2.01), and city of residence (Birmingham (ref.) v. Houston, adjusted OR = 0.20, 95% CI: 0.10, 0.39). Children in food insecure households consumed more daily servings of fruits and vegetables on average (mean = 2.44) than children in food secure households (mean = 2.16, p = 0.04). [Author Abstract]

83.) **Lee, J. S.**

Understanding targeting in the Elderly Nutrition Program: A focus of food insecurity. Ph.D. dissertation, Cornell University. 2002.

This research examined whether the current concept and measures of food insecurity have utility in targeting those elderly in need of food assistance programs, particularly Elderly Nutrition Program (ENP). Both quantitative and qualitative research methods were used to address this goal. The quantitative portion of the research used secondary data analysis to examine whether food insecurity identifies the elderly in need of food assistance programs. The qualitative part of the research used open-ended and discovery-oriented interviews to understand how targeting and the need for services are perceived and operationalized in the delivery of services in ENP. Interviews were conducted with 36 local ENP providers in six counties of Upstate New York. The current definition and measure of food insecurity used by USDA/DHHS for nutrition monitoring purposes may not be sufficient because they do not incorporate some of the unique components of food insecurity in the elderly. Specifically, the component that is missing relates to food use. Food insecurity, even as it is presently defined, indicates those who are in need of food assistance programs. Food insecure elderly experience multiple problems that compromise their nutritional status, such as poverty, low-education, minority status, and functional impairments. Furthermore, food insecurity indicates those elderly at nutritional risk. Food insecurity was significantly associated with lower nutrient intakes and skinfold thicknesses, poorer self-reported health status, and higher nutritional risk scores. This research, however, was incapable of showing the potential to benefit from program participation among food insecure elderly due to limited data and research design. The broadened concept of food insecurity is definitely an important indicator of need for food assistance programs in the elderly. However, even the expanded concept of food insecurity is not a sufficient indicator of service needs for the ENP. Local ENP providers' perceptions of need for services were rich and complex. Food insecurity only partially indicates those who are in need of the ENP. A holistic understanding of the living situation and the mental, physical, and medical conditions of the elderly are critical to a full understanding of nutritional risk of the elderly and to targeting decisions for the ENP. [Author Abstract]

84.) **Letts, E. M.**

Urban agriculture and various food sourcing strategies how can they mitigate food insecurity amongst the urban poor in Cape Town, South Africa?

M.S. thesis, Queen's University (Canada). 2013.

South Africa is considered food secure yet, depending on the source used, it is estimated that food insecurity exists in 20-52% of households. Many factors, such as differing livelihood strategies, play significant roles in determining food security and this project attempted to explore these issues, using Cape Town as a case study. In particular, we compared two types of urban agricultural interventions: home and community gardening as facilitated by two urban agriculture NGO's (Soil for Life and Abalimi, respectively). Semi-structured interviews were conducted amongst 91 participants living below the poverty line in two 'townships' in Cape Town: Langa and Khayelitsha. Twenty-five home-gardeners in Langa and 21 community-gardeners in Khayelitsha were interviewed and compared with equal numbers of non-gardeners in both areas. Data analysis showed that participants who cited community gardening as a food source were most food secure (Household Food Insecurity Access Scale [HFIAS] = 13.04), followed by Langa's home gardeners (HFIAS = 18.88), Langa's non-gardeners (HFIAS = 21.84) and finally non-gardeners in Khayelitsha (HFIAS = 22.25). Food Security for non-gardeners in Langa and Khayelitsha was correlated with income (r=0.78; 0.48, respectively), as compared to both gardening groups. The gardeners in Langa and Khayelitsha also showed more diversified diets and lower Months of Inadequate Household Food

Provisioning Scores (MIHFP), indicating fewer months of inadequate food provisioning. These data suggest that food security may be positively affected by gardening practices as well as by increased diversity in food sourcing. Community gardening appeared to be more effective than home gardening, perhaps due to greater accessibility to inputs such as land space, manure and water, as facilitated directly by the associated NGO. [Author Abstract]

85.) **Levay, A.**

The Influence of Gender and Food Insecurity on the Eating Practices of Poor, Pregnant Women in Dhaka, Bangladesh.

M.S. thesis, University of Alberta (Canada). 2012.

The purpose of this study was to investigate the interaction between rising levels of food insecurity in the urban setting and the existing gender structures and their impact on eating practices while pregnant. Using a focused-ethnography with a feminist approach in an urban slum in Dhaka, Bangladesh, we interviewed pregnant women and new mothers as well as older women, traditional midwives, delivery center staff and husbands. Knowledge around food practices while pregnant was largely in agreement with the western biomedical understanding of healthy pregnancy nutrition. However, women were largely unable to operationalize this knowledge due to poverty. Gender norms in the slum setting appear to be being challenged with respects to mobility and decision-making. However, limited access to sufficient quality and quantities of food overrode women's seemingly increased level of "freedom" in the slum. A more humanistic approach to maternal nutrition programs is proposed. [Author Abstract]

86.) **Liere, M. J. van.**

Coping with household food insecurity: a longitudinal and seasonal study among the Otammari in Northwestern Benin.

Ph.D. dissertation, Landbouwuniversiteit Wageningen (The Netherlands). 1993.

A longitudinal and seasonal study was conducted in an Otammari commune, Atacora Province, Benin, 1990-91, to examine the relationships between coping with food insecurity and socio-economic characteristics at the household level; and seasonal changes in food consumption, time allocation and nutritional status at the individual level. The data suggest that coping behaviour at household level was effective in the short term because members of households with insufficient cereal stocks did not lose more body weight than the individuals belonging to households with sufficient stocks. Households with insufficient stocks coped with insecurity by gathering wild foods, selling livestock, seasonal migration and reduction of meals. Children seemed protected in times of seasonal food insecurity by a more favourable food distribution. The findings imply that development projects to promote household food security should concentrate on strengthening existing local coping strategies rather than introducing non-indigenous innovations. [Author Abstract]

87.) **Lipman Diaz, E. G.**

Food insecurity and childhood obesity: A novel approach to measuring and disentangling the relationship.

Ph.D. dissertation, University of Miami. 2013.

In the United States, approximately 12.5 million children are obese and at subsequent risk for persistent, worsening obesity into adulthood and numerous negative health consequences. Childhood obesity rates are highest among racial/ethnic minority children, a worrisome problem given the association with the substantial number of poor health outcomes. Meanwhile, more than 16 million American children are impacted by food insecurity, a public health issue presumed to be the opposite of obesity. Food insecurity also disproportionately impacts racial/ethnic minority children. As a nutrition-related disorder, food insecurity confers significant risks to child health and well-being, one of which, paradoxically may be obesity. Some studies have shown childhood obesity to be among the consequences of food insecurity, however other studies have had contradictory results and clarity in the relationship remains elusive. Assessing two chief components of food security separately, dietary quality and dietary quantity, is one possible way to illuminate obesity risk more clearly than the traditional measurement approach of grouping nutritional quality and quantity together. The purpose of this study was to explore the relationship between food insecurity and childhood obesity by investigating food quality as a mechanism through which the relationship may exist. A secondary data analysis of the National Health and Nutrition

Examination Survey 2007-2008 cycle was conducted employing SEM methodology to compare two models of food insecurity for goodness-of-fit: (1) a combined 5-item food insecurity factor model, and (2) a 3-item food insecurity by quality factor model. Measurement invariance tests were conducted with the model of best fit to assess how the model relationship may differ by race/ethnicity and sex. The model using the three quality-related food insecurity items and BMI z-score achieved goodness of fit, however food quality did not predict BMI z-score. In the test of equivalence between minorities and non-minorities, the model fit the data, but food insecurity was not a predictor of BMI z-score and measurement invariance could not be established. Nevertheless, the factor loadings on the quality-related food insecurity items were stronger among minorities compared to non-minorities, indicating a statistically significant difference in response patterns. Measurement invariance between boys and girls also could not be established. While the results of this study did not support the approach undertaken, food quality remains a factor of interest in the relationship between food insecurity and childhood obesity given that the proposed model fit the data, and diminished food quality is associated with both food insecurity and obesity. Nurses are uniquely positioned to address the problems of food insecurity and childhood obesity through clinical, educational, political advocacy, and research-related work. The results of this study provide both a rationale and a springboard for future study. [Author Abstract]

88.) **Lofton, K. L. L.**

Examining the relationships among obesity, food insecurity, perceived stress and emotional eating.

Ph.D. dissertation, The University of Southern Mississippi. 2007.

The relationship between food insecurity and obesity is a complex issue that has become the subject of research and policy debate. Numerous studies have been published attempting to describe the relationship between food insecurity and obesity; however, causation and potential mechanisms to better understand the relationship have not been established. Therefore, the purpose of this study was to examine the hypothesized relationships among food insecurity, obesity, stress and emotional eating and to determine if stress and emotional eating serve as moderating mechanisms for the food insecurity and obesity phenomenon. A cross-sectional study consisting of a survey of 636 participants in two regional Headstart centers in South Mississippi was utilized to address the study objectives. The survey instrument consisted of a 7-item Food Security Scale, the 10-item Perceived Stress Scale, and the 25-item Emotional Eating Scale. In addition, BMI calculated from measured height and weight was used for classifying weight status. Demographic variables included self-reported heights and weights, perceived weight status, age, educational level, income, race, number of members living in the household, marital status and participation in food assistance programs. Analyses of the data revealed 84 percent of the participants were African American; approximately 53 percent had either a high school education or less; more than 75 percent of participants earned less than \$20,000 annually, while 87 percent lived in a household with at least five members. Single female head of household made up 60.5 percent of the households. A chi-square test of independence comparing women's perceptions to actual weight classification was significant ($\chi 2$ (N = 631, df = 9) = 93.22, p < .000) and further examination revealed that among participants, 45.4% of the women who perceived their weight status as normal were overweight and 76.6% of women who perceived their weight status as overweight were obese. Only 13.9 percent of obese participants perceived their weight accurately. Other interesting findings revealed approximately one-third (32.6 percent) of the participants reported fully food secure households. 26.4 percent of the participants were food insecure without hunger. The rate of food insecurity with hunger was 9.5 percent, more than twice the national average (3.9 percent). Multiple linear regression and moderation analyses were used to predict linear relationships between food insecurity, perceived stress, emotional eating and BMI of the female participants (n = 636). Among independent variables, perceived stress was the sole predictor of BMI [F (1,634) = 4.14, p = .042, R2 = .006]. There was no moderation noted between food insecurity, perceived stress, and emotional eating in relationship to BMI. Further investigation examining food insecurity, stress, emotional eating and obesity using qualitative research approaches to explore coping strategies and ethnic and cultural differences in eating behaviors may provide a more in-depth understanding of behaviors related to obesity. [Author Abstract]

89.) **Lu, J.**

Effects of biofuel policies on world food insecurity---a CGE analysis.

Ph.D. dissertation, Texas A&M University. 2011.

The food vs. fuel debate has heated up since the 2008 global food crisis when major crop prices dramatically increased. Heavily subsidized biofuel production was blamed for diverting food crops from food production and diverting resources from food and feed production, triggering a food crisis globally and leading to increases in the world food insecure population. Few studies have quantified the effects of biofuel policies on world food prices and world food insecurity. This study added the Brazil and China's biofuel sectors to an existing global trade CGE model, and applies the measurement of food insecurity as developed by FAO. Alternative scenarios were simulated to analyze the effect of U.S., Brazil, and China's biofuel policies on world food insecurity. Results are examined with focus on (1) effects on domestic biofuel productions, (2) change in food commodity productions and trade, (3) change in land use and land rents, and (4) change in regional undernourished populations. Results indicated that biofuel expansion is not cost competitive to traditional fossil fuel. Without any policy incentives, huge expansion of biofuel production is not likely under current technology. The conventional biofuel mandates in U.S., Brazil and China lead to increases in world food insecurity, while the advanced biofuel mandate in U.S. has the opposite effect. Subsidies to biofuels production help to lessen the increase in world food insecurity that is caused by increases in conventional biofuel production. Additionally, the effects from U.S. biofuel policies are smaller but more widespread than the effects from Brazil or China's biofuel policies. Overall, the long term effects of biofuel production expansion on world food insecurity are much smaller than expected. [Author Abstract]

90.) **Lweno, O.**

Food insecurity and social support as determinants of health outcomes among patients attending rural HIV clinic in Bushbuckridge, South Africa.

M.S. thesis, University of the Witwatersrand (South Africa). 2010.

Broad objectives: To determine the influence of food security and social support on the health outcomes of HIV patients attending Rixile Clinic in Tintswalo Hospital from March 2003-May 2008. Specific Objectives: • To describe the distribution of food security and social support among HIVpatients attended between March 2003 and May 2008. • To determine the health outcomes of HIV patients attended between March 2003 and May 2008. • To investigate predictors of health outcomes among selected factors that affected patients attended at Rixile Clinic between March 2003 and May 2008. [Author Abstract]

91.) **Lyons, A.**

A national view of household food insecurity: An analysis of the Canadian Community Health Survey, Cycle 2.1.

M.P.H. thesis, Lakehead University (Canada). 2006.

Food security exists when all people, at all times, have physical and economic access to sufficient, safe and nutritious food to meet their dietary needs and food preferences for an active and healthy life (Rome Deceleration of World Food Security, 1996). The most recent report on food insecurity shows that an estimated 3.7 million Canadians (14.7% of the population) nationwide experienced food insecurity in 2000-2001 (Ledrou & Gervais, 2005). Ledrou & Gervais (2005) reported seven percent of Canadians experienced the most severe form of food insecurity: they or someone in the household did not have enough to eat because of a lack of money. Since 1989, there has been an increase of more than 184, 309 hungry children and a 118% increase in the use of food banks throughout Canada (Canadian Association of Food Banks, 2005). Canada recognized the importance of food security in April 2005 by voting in favour of the UN Commission on Human Rights 'right to food resolution'. This pledge supports a previous commitment that includes Canada's signing of The Rome Declaration on World Food Security along with 186 other countries in 1996. Signing this non-binding treaty galvanized the Canadian government into action and resulted in the creation of Canada's Action Plan for Food Security (1998) and a government branch called the Food Security Bureau. However, after several years, food security conditions have failed to improve throughout

Canada. Food security is recognized as an important determinant of health (McIntyre, 2004; Public Health Agency of Canada, 2005). Numerous studies note the relationship between inadequate nutrient intake, poor health and food insecurity. A growing body of empirical research examining the negative associations between food insecurity and well-being signifies the emergence of food security as a public health concern. Further, the negative cost externalities associated with the effects of food insecurity may contribute to rising health care costs. In order to improve the health of Canadians, it is imperative that conditions of food insecurity throughout the country are well understood. A population health approach, addressing determinants of health such as food insecurity has the potential to reduce material and social inequalities within the population and improve overall health outcomes (Public Health Agency of Canada, 2005). For these reasons, the following research questions are examined: (1) What is the prevalence and distribution of household food insecurity in Canada? (2) What associations exist between household food insecurity and household level sociodemographic characteristics? (3) What associations exist between household food insecurity and individual level socio demographic and other selected characteristics? (4) What is the likelihood of experiencing selected health outcomes based on each dimension of household food insecurity status? The conceptual framework developed for this research encompasses both household and individual level characteristics, and seeks to establish relationships among these variables, food insecurity and health outcomes (Figure 1.1). The variables included in this model are of interest because of their previously documented relationships with food insecurity and hypothesized associations (Che and Chen, 2001; Rainville and Brink, 2001:Vozoris and Tarasuk, 2003). Household level socio-demographic characteristics and individual level characteristics are examined as potential explanatory variables for household level food insecurity. Household food insecurity is measured via four different dimensions: food insecure, compromised diet, food anxiety and food poverty. Each dimension is then examined in relation to selected health outcomes. The body of this analysis contains five sections. A thorough review of the food security literature outlines background topics such as the socio-political context of food insecurity in Canada as well as the conceptualization of food security. A chronological evaluation of the tools used to measure food insecurity is conducted and the current gold standard measure is reviewed. Results of the analysis are then presented to showcase the associations of food insecurity in relation to sociodemographic, health and psychosocial characteristics. Research findings are discussed relative to the research questions answered and those that are raised. [Author Abstract]

92.) **Maes, K. C.**

Examining social determinants of food insecurity, common mental disorders, and motivations among AIDS care volunteers in urban Ethiopia during the 2008 food crisis. Ph.D. dissertation, Emory University. 2010.

By mixing ethnographic and community-based epidemiological methods, this dissertation aims to illuminate the challenges facing AIDS care volunteers in urban Ethiopia, a setting characterized by low income, high rates of food insecurity, and ongoing scale-up of highly-active antiretroviral therapy programs. Shortages of health workers--widely recognized as the greatest threat to global health--are addressed throughout sub-Saharan Africa by using community volunteers. Whether it is unjust and/or unsustainable to rely on volunteerism in such settings has become a major concern for a widening group of social scientists and global health practitioners. This dissertation demonstrates that acute-on-chronic food insecurity during the 2008 global food crisis impacted psychosocial health and motivations to continue volunteering among AIDS care volunteers serving local non-governmental organizations in Addis Ababa, Ethiopia. This dissertation also proposes a theory of how volunteers' pro-social motivations are shaped and sustained by local norms of reciprocity and empathy, as well as by global group rituals organized by the institutions that rely on volunteer labor in rolling out antiretroviral therapies in settings of chronic food insecurity. Participant observation was conducted in neighborhoods adjacent to a large public hospital in southwest Addis Ababa, including attendance at volunteer trainings, caregiver and care recipient homes, volunteers' reporting and planning meetings, and volunteer recognition ceremonies, over 20 months between May 2007 and January 2009. A purposive sample of 13 volunteer caregivers was recruited to complete a series of semi-structured open-ended interviews. In addition, a random sample of 110 volunteers from two local NGOs was surveyed 3 times over 11 months in 2008. Surveys included measures of food insecurity and common mental disorders, care relationship quality, and motivations for being an AIDS care volunteer. Text analyses, regression analyses, and cultural consensus analyses were triangulated to test hypotheses and interpret results. Results indicate that volunteers faced unrelenting poverty, but they also built positive, empathic relationships with others in their communities. They also expected divine rewards as Orthodox Christians caring for marginalized people. Nevertheless, this dissertation concludes that "volunteerism" is an optimistic and loaded term that oversimplifies the motivations of low-income individuals and potentially masks a system of unsustainable labor exploitation within AIDS treatment and other development-focused movements. [Author Abstract]

93.) **Mahapa, S. F.**

Rural women, food insecurity and survival strategies the Babina-Chuene Wome's Multi-purpose Project in Bochum (Northern Province).

M.S. thesis, University of Pretoria (South Africa). 2001.

In this study, the problem of food insecurity among rural women is examined. The study focuses on the food security project known as the Babina-Chuene Women's Multi-purpose Project, in Vergelegen village in the Bocum District in the Northern Province. The discussion of the food security project uses information from a literature study and data from personal interviews and questionnaires. The context of the project, background and environment of the people in the project are examined. The Study aims to find out whether this project solves the poverty and food insecurity problem in Bochum. The project is evaluated using criteria for projects in terms of project management, planning, implementation and evaluation. The project is found to meet most of the criteria, but reveals some problems that endanger its sustainability. Some recommendations are made. [Author Abstract]

94.) **Maroto, M. E.**

Food insecurity among community college students: Prevalence and relationship to GPA, energy, and concentration.

Ed.D. dissertation, Morgan State University. 2013.

The latest U.S. government surveys indicate that one in six Americans suffer from food insecurity, which means they have trouble affording adequate food. Previous research has shown that food insecurity affects adult cognitive ability, energy levels, ability to concentrate as well as child academic success. Food insecurity has been studied in college students at 4-year institutions; however, research on the community college population is sparse. This study aimed to better understand the extent and implications of food insecurity among community college students attending two community colleges in Maryland. The research was carried out using a survey that collected data related to student food insecurity, demographics, along with self-reported Grade Point Average (GPA), energy, and concentration levels in 301 community college students. Approximately half of the students attended a suburban community college (n=151) and half of the students attended an urban community college (n=150). Data from each school were compared to examine issues affecting students attending each institution. The study revealed that over half of the community college student respondents were food insecure and that food insecurity was slightly less prevalent among respondents at the suburban community than those from the urban community college. African American students and multiracial students were more likely to experience food insecurity than White students. Students who lived alone, with roommates or with spouses/partners were more likely to experience food insecurity than students who lived with parents or relatives. Single parents were also more likely to be food insecure than students who were not single parents. Food insecurity was significantly associated with student GPA, energy, and concentration in the overall student sample. Food insecure students were more likely to fall into a lower GPA category than they were to fall into the highest GPA category. Food insecure students were also more likely to report lower energy and concentration levels and the degree of food insecurity appeared to affect the probability of low energy or difficulty concentrating. When considering each community college separately, food insecurity was significantly associated with GPA at the suburban community college but not at the urban community college. Also, food insecurity had a stronger association with energy and concentration at the urban community college than at the suburban community college. [Author Abstract]

95.) **McGuire, M.**

Poverty, food insecurity and overweight/obesity in the Canadian population.

M.Sc. thesis, University of Ottawa (Canada). 2007.

This study, based on the Canadian Community Health Survey (2004), examined the relationship between food insecurity and overweight/obesity among Canadian adults by sex and family type using logistic regression analysis; we also provided an environmental scan of policies, programs and initiatives to address food insecurity. In our final adjusted models, food insecure women with hunger were significantly more likely to be overweight/obese than food secure women [OR=2.3, CI=1.2, 4.3]. Our environmental scan revealed broad recognition of the importance of addressing food insecurity and concrete recommendations to do so. We found far less recognition of the implications of food insecurity for healthy weights within a policy context. The food insecurity/overweight/obesity relationship and its policy implications are complex; we need a better understanding of how underlying social and economic conditions, sex, and family type relate to income, food security and healthy weights. [Author Abstract]

96.) **McNeill, K.**

Talking with their mouths half full food insecurity in the Hamilton community. Ph.D. dissertation, University of Waikato (New Zealand). 2011.

While the sociology of food has attended to what symbolisms of presence can tell us about society, the same attention has not been attributed to symbolisms of absence. Within the context of affluent post-industrial societies, food insecurity means that people are "at times, uncertain of having, or unable to acquire, enough food for all household members because they had insufficient money and other resources for food" (Nord et al. 2009, p. 2). This project is a comprehensive study of responses to, and experiences of, food insecurity in Hamilton City. The issue of food insecurity has been difficult to politicise in New Zealand. One of the reasons for this is that the demand for food aid is usually reported by individual organisations, rather than across the entire food support sector. The first phase of this research was a multi-provider survey that documented the demand for formal food support in Hamilton over a one year period in 2006/2007. The findings show that during this time the community absorbed $1,157,623 worth of state funded Special Needs Grants for Food, while philanthropically funded third sector organisations provided 4,232 food parcels and 25,557 community meals. The survey findings demonstrate that the socio-political environment in which formal food support takes place is characterised by the unwillingness of the state to fully realise its role in affirming the right of citizens to be free from hunger. At the same time, there is evidence of a corresponding willingness to delegate provision of food aid to charity based third sector organisations that receive no state funding. The second phase of the study was a qualitative exploration of the experiences of ten community members who were confirmed as food insecure using the 'Standard 6-item Indicator to Classifying Households by Food Security Status' (Bickel et al., 2000). The data showed that, as far as they were able, respondents exercised a range of endogenous strategies (the means that individuals and households applied in the private domain to manage food insecurity and hunger), but ultimately, the utility of these diminished. In this event, respondents pursued either informal exogenous strategies (through social networks), or, particularly where there were limitations on social capital, formal exogenous strategies in the form of service use. This study points to food insecurity as an experience that is shrouded with secrecy, shame and fear of stigma. Further, the experience carries with it a range of social implications in the form of exclusion, marginalisation and disempowerment, all of which have seldom been recognised elsewhere in the literature. In acknowledging the complex and non-linear nature of food insecurity at macro, meso and micro levels, Rittel and Webber's (1973) criteria for 'wicked problems' is utilised as a theoretical framework for synthesising the findings. The thesis advocates for a collaborative approach to re-solving the persistence of food insecurity in which the range of stakeholders involved is broadened to include those who 'talk with their mouths half full'. [Author Abstract]

97.) **Melcarek, H. G.**

An examination of three California urban garden organizations: An activist response to food insecurity.

Ph.D. dissertation, University of California, Santa Cruz. 2009.

Food security, or sustained access to nutritious food from non-emergency sources, is one of humanity's most basic needs. However, it is beyond the reach of large segments of the population, especially in low-income, of-color, and single mother households. In urban agriculture lies the potential to lessen the effects of poverty, improve food security, empower individuals and communities, introduce participants to organic and agroecological growing practices, and beautify and green neighborhoods. Using an interdisciplinary approach, I examined the growing practices and goals related to inclusion, empowerment, and food security of urban garden organizations in low-income communities of color in a major metropolitan area of California. I used open-ended, semi-structured interviews, participant observation, demographic surveys, content analysis, botanical censuses, and garden mapping to collect both social and natural science data in three case studies of urban garden organizations with sustainable agriculture and social justice goals. The organizations in this study ascribed to various tenets of the environmental justice, community food security, and food justice movements, which provide frameworks for empowering urban-based, low-income people of color to obtain sufficient, fair access to resources--be those resources a clean environment, healthy food, or both. However, these movements work toward these goals in various ways and with different emphases. I describe how urban garden organizations utilize the frameworks and goals of these movements, and how these various frameworks affect their outcomes. I find that organizations that use a food justice approach are well situated to improve food security and change power structures in low-income inner-city neighborhoods. Food justice organizations in this study focused on goals related to inclusion and empowerment of community members, planted proportionately more edible crops, planted on a higher percentage of their land, grew primarily culturally appropriate crops, and one organization hired directly from the food-insecure community that it served. I provide recommendations for urban garden organizations in general to improve participation, diversity, and agroecological sustainability in their organizations and in the food system as a whole. [Author Abstract]

98.) **Mendoza, R. M.**

Towards a biocultural approach a review of food insecurity, low income, and obesity in the United States.

M.A. thesis, University of Georgia. 2007.

Currently the United States and other industrialized nations are experiencing the stark impact of a global nutrition transition through a radical and national increase in obesity rates. The increasing presentation of this disease, however, is concentrated in food insecure, and low-income populations. Research that has examined the etiology of this correlation has approached this relationship from either a biological approach, or an economic approach. The literature presented by both camps, however, is unable to fully elucidate the presentation of obesity in these populations. Instead this review argues for the integration of these perspectives in a biocultural approach that addresses how structural inequalities work in conjunction with human biological processes, and cultural coping mechanisms to affect national obesity distributions. [Author Abstract]

99.) **Minkoff-Zern, L.**

Migrations of Hunger and Knowledge: Food Insecurity and California's Indigenous Farmworkers.

Ph.D. dissertation, University of California, Berkeley. 2012.

This dissertation explores two elements of farmworker food insecurity in California, the structural conditions of food insecurity, and the use of immigrant/cross-border agricultural and culinary knowledge as coping strategies. The first component, structural and systemic causes for farmworker food insecurity, investigates how farmworker food insecurity is linked to international trade and immigration policies, as well as the historical exploitation of people of color in California's agricultural sector. Rather than simply chronicle a story of exploited laboring bodies, I expand upon on this narrative, exploring the ways that indigenous Oaxacan farmworkers, who for the most part come from a culture deeply rooted in food and agricultural practices, cope with food insecurity by utilizing their embodied agricultural and nutritional knowledge. I explore the linkages between their place in the food system as both producers and consumers, as they are simultaneously exploited for their labor, and creating coping mechanisms using their culinary and agricultural experience. [Author Abstract]

100.) **Misselhorn, A. A.**

Food insecurity in Southern Africa: Causes and emerging response options from evidence at regional, provincial and local scales.

Ph.D. dissertation, University of the Witwatersrand (South Africa). 2007.

The overarching objective of this thesis is to determine causes of food insecurity in southern Africa, and how it can best be addressed. This objective is addressed through a number of research questions and methods at three geographic scales: the regional, through a technique of meta-analysis which is used to synthesise 49 local-level household economy case studies; the provincial, through a Delphi panel of practitioner experience; and the local, using multiple research techniques, including participatory methods. An extremely diverse range of factors contributing to food-insecurity are found at all three scales, indicating that community- and household-specific dynamics give rise to forms of food insecurity. Two common processes, however, are argued to be common across all the case study communities in the regional-scale research. These are the closely related processes of cycles of intensifying vulnerability associated with livelihood trade-offs, and of community level social capital changing into forms that undermine resilience to food insecurity - such as the decline in two-parent families. A further probing of social capital at the local level suggests that while social capital takes multiple forms, and further remains in many respects a problematic concept, it nevertheless provides a valuable lens through which powerful social dynamics might be examined in developing responses to food insecurity. Policy makers and change agents should carefully consider their role in building community social-capital that might enhance the ability of vulnerable communities to overcome livelihood constraints and adapt to the tremendous challenges posed by changing economic environments in southern Africa. Drawing on the research at all scales, a framework is provided that calls for a reconceptualisation of food-security interventions to focus on intervention processes, applicable at all scales and in all contexts across the region. [Author Abstract]

101.) **Moyo, P.**

Urban food insecurity, coping strategies and resistance in Bulawayo, Zimbabwe. Ph.D. dissertation, University of Leeds (United Kingdom). 2009.

This thesis examines urban food insecurity and attendant coping strategies employed by the urban poor in Makokoba and Mzilikazi in Bulawayo in the face of Zimbabwe's 2001-2007 national food insecurity and unprecedented economic recession. The thesis argues that even though Zimbabwe's rural areas remain the locus of poverty and food insecurity compared to urban areas, there is evidence that since 2000 an increase in urban poverty made urban food insecurity primarily a problem of access by the urban poor. Hyperinflation pushed up food prices, eroded the purchasing power of poor households. The urban poor's overarching strategy was to construct and maintain a portfolio of coping strategies which concurrently alleviated household food gaps. These relied not only on consumption austerity measures, trade-based, production, own-labour and inheritance/transfer entitlements within and beyond the urban hinterland but also increasing straddling of the rural-urban divide. The thesis examines whether state responses to the national food emergency that include direct government intervention in domestic food markets and its channelling of food into public social safety nets complemented the urban poor's coping strategies. It finds that not only did state intervention in the food market largely exacerbate urban food shortages but its social safety net system was beleaguered by underfunding, programmatic, technical, means testing and organisational inefficiencies that undermined its contribution to the urban poor's coping strategies. It also identifies how politics was used to control food distributed through the social safety net system; with widespread appropriation along partisan ZANU-PF political party lines and the exclusion of non-ZANU-PF members. [Author Abstract]

102.) **Munemo, N.**

Politics during dry times: Incumbent insecurity and the provision of drought relief in contemporary Africa.

Ph.D. dissertation, Columbia University. 2008.

Since gaining independence, a number of African governments have responded to protect citizens from drought-induced threats of famine. Government relief has generally involved limited disbursements of food aid and large income restoring labor-intensive public works program for the able bodied (labor-based relief) or the universal distribution of free food aid (free food aid). By demonstrating that the choice of drought relief involves non-trivial trade-offs between economic effectiveness and political gain, I argue that variation in the form taken by government relief programs can be explained by incumbent insecurity. The dissertation shows that when incumbents are faced with immediate threats to their position and power they are more likely to rely on political supporters to design and implement drought relief programs. This deference to political clients in the choice of relief leads to the adoption of free food aid by insecure incumbents. [Author Abstract]

103.) **Musi, P. J.**

Coping with food and income insecurity: The case of Swazi households.

Ph.D. dissertation, University of Illinois at Urbana-Champaign. 1993.

This study investigates two related issues of development, economic well-being and micro-level adjustments used by households to deal with food insecurity. Specifically the study (a) describes the food security situation of households in the Middleveld and Lowveld areas of Swaziland, (b) determines the strategies used by households to mitigate against food insecurity and how these vary by household characteristics and area of residence, and (c) describes the scope of nongovernmental programs designed to assist households to deal with food and income insecurity. Qualitative and quantitative data for this study were collected from a random sample of 260 households and personnel from nongovernmental agencies. Four measures of food and income security were used: (a) self-sufficiency in maize, (b) per capita income, (c) quality of diet, and (d) subjective food ranking. The results of this study suggest that area of residence rather than household characteristics is the more important determinant of the household's food security. Households in the Middleveld showed higher levels of food security than those from the Lowveld, and the effect of being in a rural development area was insignificant. Periurban households had higher levels of income and food security than rural households. The effect on food and income security of gender of household head, age composition of household, marital status of the principal woman of the household, ownership of durable goods, and number of cattle owned varied by the measure used. Income diversification, crop diversification, using available wild food, and reducing the number of meals consumed per day were the coping strategies most commonly adopted. The hypotheses that Lowveld households would have higher levels of income and food production diversification were not supported, but Lowveld households did use more consumption strategies than Middleveld households. The results of multiple regression showed that marital status, age composition of household, total household income, amount of land farmed, number of resident adult females, gender of household head, age of respondent, ownership of durable goods, and household size were associated with the extent of use of the different coping strategies. There was evidence that the immediate environment is no longer a significant food source whereas remittances are increasingly playing an important role in securing food consumption during drought-induced food shortages. The study concludes with research questions generated by the findings of the study. [Author Abstract]

104.) **Mykerezi, E.**

Three essays on the well-being of vulnerable populations.

Ph.D. dissertation, Virginia Polytechnic Institute and State University. 2007.

This dissertation is composed of three essays that measure the impact of social programs and policies on the wellbeing of their target populations. The first essay entitled "The Wage Impact of Historically Black College and University Attendance" examines the impact of attending a Historically Black College or University on the wages of Blacks attending HBCUs versus other four year colleges or universities using a sample of Blacks from the National Longitudinal Survey of Youth (1979). The study finds no initial advantage to HBCU attendance for black men, but a 1.4 to 1.6 percentage point higher growth rate in subsequent wages is associated with the attendance of an HBCU as opposed to other four year colleges. This faster growth rate translates in a net discounted HBCU earnings gain of 8.9 to 9.6 percent over a 16 year period following college attendance. The study finds no advantage or disadvantage to HBCU attendance for Black females. The second essay entitled "Transient and Chronic Poverty in the US: The Role of the Food Stamp Program" examines the unique and common determinants of short-term intra-annual transient poverty and chronic poverty, as well as the differential response of each state of poverty to Food Stamp Program (FSP) use. The study employs dynamic expenditure-based poverty measures using quarterly data from the Consumer Expenditure Survey (2001-2004). The major finding is that FSP use reduces transient poverty, but the study finds no significant impact of FSP use on chronic poverty. The common causes of both states of poverty are low human capital, minority status and involuntary unemployment of the household head. Changes in family composition during the year is only associated with higher transient poverty. The third essay entitled "Food Insecurity and the Food Stamp Program" examines the determinants of food insecurity in the US, as well as its response to Food Stamp Program use with data from the Panel Study of Income Dynamics (1995-1999). The study finds that FSP use reduces household food insecurity, and that the program impact is greater for households that experience more severe insecurity. In addition the study finds that higher risk tolerance as well as a preference for smoking cigarettes increase household food insecurity. [Author Abstract]

105.) **Nanama, S.**

Experience, trends, and consequences of food insecurity in complex households in rural Burkina Faso.

Ph.D. dissertation, Cornell University. 2005.

The household is often considered as the smallest group of persons living together, and commonly making decisions about production and consumption. Under this assumption, food insecurity programs have focused on the household as a unit of intervention. In places where social structure is complex, experience food insecurity is likely to vary among household members. Understanding food insecurity and its consequences in these complex settings is relevant to policy making. To understand the difference in the experience of food insecurity between household's members, manly men and women, we conducted a qualitative in-depth study with 33 people including men and women form 10 households. In addition, we designed and implemented a follow-up of 126 complex households in rural Burkina Faso. We collected data twice every year, during the post-harvest season and the hungry season. A total of Five waves of data collection were completed. The data includes demographic characteristics, household wealth, food intake, anthropometry, and food security using experience-based questionnaires. The qualitative data were analyzed following the principle of theme analysis. Correlation, mixed regression models and path analysis were used on the quantitative data to describe the trend of food insecurity, examine the relation between household and mother-children sub-units food insecurity, and investigate the effect of food insecurity on women's health and their caring practices. We found that men experience food insecurity differently than women and that the difference was more related to the difference in their role within the household. We also found that the mother-children sub-unit's food insecurity was related to household food insecurity in a positive way and that, factors such as woman's rank and marital status modifies the relationship. Finally, we showed that food insecurity was associated with poor nutritional status and with poor caring practices in women. These findings suggest that, in the study context and in similar contexts, priority in targeting should be given to polygamous households that are typically more food insecure than are monogamous households, and to mother-children sub-units that are less likely to benefit from an improved access to food by household heads. In addition, these interventions should take into account the possibility of non-nutrition-related consequences of food insecurity. [Author Abstract]

106.) **Nguyen, T. G.**

Food insecurity and the evolution of indigenous risk sharing institutions in the Sahel. Ph.D. dissertation, The Ohio State University. 1998.

In semi-arid Africa, income fluctuations pose a critical problem of food security for rural households. In the absence of complete insurance markets, households have developed a broad range of market and non-market institutions to smooth their consumption. Standard neoclassical economic theories predict that in the presence of a complete market for state-contingent claims, transfers are made across individuals so that individual consumption responds to aggregate income shocks only. A formal test of the perfect risk-sharing was conducted using household panel data from Burkina Faso. The null hypothesis of perfect risk-sharing was rejected at the 5 percent significance level. Further statistical analyses were undertaken to classify households along a consumption scale. Results also showed that extended households offer better insurance coverage than nuclear households by state-contingent contracts and intertemporal transfers, and that family labor and the size of livestock herd are positively correlated with the household's level of food consumption. Starting from a situation where all nuclear households are organized in extended households, the current picture of agro-pastoral economies displays an apparent disfunctional social insurance scheme. A static stochastic semi-cooperative model of an extended household was derived to show that the extended household viewed as a risk-sharing institution is not sustainable for certain conditions. Simulation results suggested that nuclear households improve their welfare by participating in the household risk-sharing scheme, but that large aggregate shocks and unequal endowments of labor and assets reduce significantly the space of feasible insurance contracts. A dynamic version of the same household model was then developed and solved using the Chebychev polynomial projection method to capture the time dimension of consumption smoothing. When households are heterogeneous, unequal endowments of labor and assets and unequal redistribution of common surpluses give the better-endowed member an incentive to either leave the household or to shirk by accumulating less resources in the long run and consuming more today. The decline of traditional insurance institutions is a critical issue due to the individualized effects of this disappearance on household welfare, in an environment where well functioning markets and public interventions are rare. [Author Abstract]

107.) **Noel, J. J.**

The relationship of caregiver and household factors to weight status of American Indian preschool children.

Ph.D. dissertation, The Johns Hopkins University. 2003.

Obesity affects American Indian (AI) adults and children in higher proportions than any other group in the United States. Environmental factors appear to be the main determinant, however no study to date has explored how these factors are associated with obesity in Apache preschool children. The objective of this cross-sectional study was to examine the relationship of caregiver and household factors to weight status of Apache preschool children and their female caregivers living on the White Mountain Apache reservation in Eastern Arizona. A total of 154 women and 154 children were included in this study. Anthropometric measurements of height (cm), weight (kg), subscapular (mm) and triceps (mm) were conducted with children and caregivers. The Child Feeding Questionnaire (CFQ) was used to evaluate the caregivers' child-feeding practices. A qualitative food frequency questionnaire was used to assess dietary patterns of the children. Demographic and socio-economic information were collected from an interviewer-administered questionnaire with caregivers. The Radimer/Cornell measure was used to assess the prevalence and severity of food insecurity. Over 23% of Apache preschool-aged children were overweight (BMI ≥; 95th), and over 25% were at risk of overweight (BMI 85th -95th). Apache children were significantly heavier their age- and gender matched reference (BMI z-score +1.0 ± 09; p < 0.001). Sixty-seven percent of Apache women were obese (BMI ≥ 30) and 24% were overweight (BMI 25-30). Children were nearly 4 times more likely to be overweight if their caregiver was obese (OR = 3.95; 95% CI, 1.6-10.1). Over 79% of the study participants experienced food insecurity; 35% were household food insecure, 16% were adult food insecure and 28% of children in Apache households experienced hunger. Food insecurity was not associated with BMI of preschool children or their female caregivers. Specific variables associated with hunger and food insecurity in multivariate analyses were: less household income, less education of caregiver, younger age of caregiver and food stamp participation. Multivariate models were used to examine significant predictors of controlling feeding practices. Food insecurity was a significant predictor of pressuring children to eat more food and restricting children from consuming high fat foods in this sample. There was a significant inverse relationship between pressure to eat and the following variables: perception of a child's weight, caregiver's education, and caregiver's age. Concern about a child becoming overweight was positively associated with restricting a child from consuming high fat foods. Multiple regression analysis showed even after controlling for household and caregiver characteristics, BMI of caregiver, child's birth weight, and frequency of consumption of foods, pressure to eat and restriction were significantly associated with BMI of Apache preschool age children. Future research is needed to examine the relationship of food insecurity and child feeding practices to weight status of AI children. [Author Abstract]

108.) **Nugent, M. A.**

Journeys to the food bank: Exploring the experience of food insecurity among postsecondary students.

M.Sc. thesis, University of Lethbridge (Canada). 2012.

Food insecurity is a global issue giving rise to health inequities affecting populations at all life stages. Postsecondary student food insecurity exists, yet is an understudied phenomenon. To provide insight into the perspectives and experiences of food insecurity in the postsecondary population, university students (n=15) who accessed a campus food bank were interviewed utilizing person-centered interviewing. The social determinants of health (SDH) and structural violence theory provided conceptual guidance for the qualitative study. Students were found to lead complex lives, shouldering many responsibilities. They valued their health however, they lacked the necessary supports to maintain adequate nutritional intake. They employed multiple strategies to mitigate their food insecurity issues, while concurrently making sacrifices and experiencing suffering. Three economic pathways leading students to food bank use included shortfall, cumulative and catastrophic pathways. This research offers increased understanding of food insecurity in this vulnerable population, exposing inequities which must be addressed. Keywords: postsecondary student, food insecurity, social determinants of health, structural violence, food bank [Author Abstract]

109.) **Nunnery, D.**

Liberians living in the U.S.: An examination of post-resettlement food insecurity and associated factors.

M.S. thesis, The University of North Carolina, Greensboro. 2012.

Objectives: To examine post-resettlement food insecurity rate and its relationship with socio-demographic and pre-resettlement characteristics among Liberian households; and assess differences in the amount of money spent on food per month by household characteristics. Design: Semi-structured in-home interviews. Setting: Southeast region of the US. Subjects: Liberian women caring for children 12 years of age or younger (n = 33). Results: Participants have lived in the US for 12 years on average. Food insecurity of any level was indicated in 61 % of households and child hunger or severe food insecurity was reported in 30 % of households. Food insecurity was higher among women who were aged 40 or older, had high school or less education and those making less than $1000 per month. Women who had arrived in the US older than 15 years of age were more likely to be food insecure. On average, participants spent $109 monthly on groceries per household member. In estimating differences, results indicated that older women, those who experienced food insecurity and did not have a car spent more money on food than their counterparts ($P \leq .10$). Conclusions: Liberian women experience high levels of food insecurity upon resettlement. Besides poor economic conditions, pre-resettlement characteristics such as number of years in refugee camps and age upon arrival (school age vs. older than school age) were associated with food security status. These findings call for future research to further understand what role pre-resettlement living conditions and experiences affect food choices, budgeting and thereby food security status among refugees. [Author Abstract]

110.) **Palko, R.**

The impact of food insecurity on nutritional status and disease progression in people living with HIV/AIDS in southeast Texas.

M.S. thesis, Lamar University, Beaumont. 2012.

The purpose of this study was to identify the impact of food insecurity on nutritional status and disease progression in people living with HIV/AIDS in Southeast Texas. Participants (N = 54) consisted of client volunteers from Triangle AIDS Network, a local non-profit HIV/AIDS clinic. Food insecurity was measured using the USDA food security status questionnaire. Indicators of nutritional status and disease progression, as well as demographic information, were obtained from the clients' medical records. Sixty-one percent (n = 33) of participants were classified as food insecure. Mean albumin levels were significantly higher in the food secure group (4.1 vs. 3.7) (p = 0.006), as compared to the food insecure group. Mean CD4 cell counts (578 vs. 409) (p = 0.042) were also higher in the food secure participants. Study findings suggest that food insecure people living with HIV/AIDS may be at risk for poorer nutritional status and more rapid disease progression than those who are food secure. [Author Abstract]

111.) **Panaguiton, Z. L. G.**

Is food insecurity a contributing factor to childhood obesity? The association of household food insecurity and obesity prevalence among children and adolescents in the United States.

M.P.H. thesis, Virginia Commonwealth University. 2010.

The obesity epidemic is a major public health concern, where the prevalence rates amongst the American children population have more than doubled since the 1980s. Among overweight children, the risk of becoming an overweight or obese adult is 70% higher than children of normal weight, and obese children are more likely to remain obese into adulthood and face a number of morbidities associated with it, including lower quality of life and increased financial burden. In this research, we examined the relationship between household food security and obesity among children and adolescents between the ages of 2-18 years old. We used data from the NHANES 2005-2006 (n= 3,432). Amongst the children aged 2-18 years, 31.21% were determined to be obese or at-risk for obesity. Children aged 2-18 years were 1.27 times more likely to be obese or at-risk when living in a food insecure household after adjusting for race/ethnicity. Adolescents aged 12-18 years were 1.47 times more likely to be obese or at-risk when living in a food insecure household. No significant association was found for young children aged 2-11 years. After adjusting for race/ethnicity and poverty level status, however, the association between food insecurity and obesity was not significant for either age group. Further investigation of other potential confounders could explain the association for both young children and adolescents. There are other factors, like social and societal, that influence the trends of obesity. Future programming could work to ameliorate the conditions of food insecurity and other infrastructure factors. [Author Abstract]

112.) **Patrick, S. S.**

A study of food insecurity and rural development in the Gambia: The impact of rural weekly markets (Lumos).

Ph.D. dissertation, Kansas State University. 2009.

Food insecurity poses an enormous challenge and is a matter of extreme urgency for The Gambia, where more than half of the population lives below the poverty line. Although extensive research confirms the problems of food insecurity in Africa, no research has concurrently advanced a bottom-up and top-down neo-endogenous theoretical framework to explore (1) the dynamics of food insecurity in The Gambia and (2) the extent to which measures used to combat it have had a positive impact. The current research aims to fill this gap by employing concurrent triangulation (mixed) methods that incorporate primary and secondary data sources. As envisaged by the neo-endogenous approach, structured interviews with participants in the weekly rural markets/ Lumo(s), underscore the crucial role this indigenous marketing system plays. This marketing system embeds socioeconomic activities in rural territories through the utilization of social and cultural capital that reduce transaction costs involved in direct marketing. Consequently this initiative increases Wassu community's access to food and stabilizes the food supply. The results also reveal moderate effects of various interventions, particularly in the Western and North Bank divisions, where agricultural production of various crops and livestock has improved the livelihood of those rural communities. At the local level, the allocation of a greater proportion of arable land to coarse grain production along with the decline in peanut production hold great promise for reducing the problem of food insecurity. Although food insecurity still prevails in much of rural Gambia as indicated by the scale of stunting among children under age five, measures are being taken to address the problem. Combined with intervention projects and other developmental effects, the potential for the Lumo(s) to reverse food insecurity in the country is great, contingent upon the central government and international lending agencies' devolution of significant powers and transfer of funds directly to rural territories. [Author Abstract]

113.) **Patton-Lopez, M. M.**

Out-of-Pocket Health Care Expenditures and Household Food Insecurity among Families with Children.

Ph.D. dissertation, Oregon State University. 2013.

Since the late 1990s accelerated growth in health care spending coupled with a cost shift of health insurance from employers to employees has created an increased financial burden for many families. Past research suggests that financial burden due to out-of-pocket (OOP) health care costs limits access to health care and may reduce spending on other basic needs, such as food. The primary objective of this study was to assess the relationship between out-of-pocket health care expenditures and food insecurity among families with children. Secondarily, this study examined the relationship between the health status of children and household food security. This study used data from the Panel Study of Income Dynamics (PSID, 2003) to test whether higher out of pocket health care expenditures increase household food insecurity for families with children. Respondents reported out of pocket expenditures for both medical services and insurance premiums in 2001 and 2002. Food insecurity was measured for the previous 12 months using the 18-item USDA Food Security Survey Module. Multivariate weighted logit analysis was conducted to model the relationship between OOP health care costs and household food security status; and child health status and household food security. There was no evidence that higher OOP health care costs were associated with household food insecurity. However, among families earning less than 300 percent of the federal poverty threshold, having private insurance did increase the likelihood of experiencing food insecurity (OR =4.77, 95% CI = 0.05 - 1.02). Households with a child in poor health were not more likely to experience food insecurity; however having a wife in poor health was ásociated with food insecurity (OR = 4.00, 95% CI =1.67- 9.52). The findings from this study suggest that programs designed to limit OOP health care spending among moderate and low income families should evaluate the impact on household food security. [Author Abstract]

114.) **Pearson, E.**

Seasonal Incomes and Food Insecurity in Rural Costa Rica: Food Consumption Patterns, Availability and Access.

M.A. thesis, University of Ottawa (Canada). 2013.

This study is based on ethnographic research that was conducted in the villages of Santa María de Rivas and San Gerardo de Rivas in the coffee farming region of Pérez Zeledón, Costa Rica. While these two villages are in close proximity to each other, the economy of San Gerardo is based more on tourism than the economy of Santa María, although both towns still engage in agricultural activities. Within each village, I conducted 15 preliminary interviews, followed by ten follow-up interviews with the main food preparers of the households. From in depth discussions, I found that food consumption patterns of people in both towns were being affected by seasonal variations in incomes due to the cyclical nature of employment in both tourism and agriculture. A number of households from these villages were experiencing periods of food worries throughout the year that were linked to the seasonality of tourism as well as agriculture, and in particular coffee production. Seasonal availability of particular food items also shaped consumption patterns; however, perceptions of food insecurity in this context appear to be primarily related to problems of access. [Author Abstract]

115.) **Pearson, R. L.**

Exploring Certified Health Education Specialists' knowledge of household food insecurity and related workforce readiness.

Ph.D. dissertation, University of Arkansas. 2008.

Food insecurity, or "limited or uncertain availability of nutritionally adequate and safe foods or limited or uncertain ability to acquire acceptable foods in socially acceptable ways," has been recognized as a problem within the United States since the 1990s. Nearly 11% of American households experienced food access issues in 2006, and the negative long-term physical, mental, and social impacts--especially for children--have been well-documented. Despite the growing depth of our understanding of food insecurity and its continuous increase in this country over the last several years, the extent to which Certified Health Education Specialists (CHES) and other community and public health professionals are aware of, receive training in, and incorporate food security strategies into their practice are unknown. CHES and other community and public health professionals have codes of ethics that would accommodate purposeful inclusion of food security strategies and research into professional practice; however, little research on food insecurity and even less regarding programs to improve food security has been conducted by these professionals. This study was designed to determine what CHES know, believe, and do about household food insecurity. All CHES with a valid email address listed in the database held by the National Commission for Health Education Credentialing were invited to participate in an online survey regarding food insecurity.

Approximately 27% completed the survey. Results indicate that participants know that many U.S. households face food access issues and that most believe that access to food is a basic human right, but that they may not be familiar with the term food insecurity. Most participants believed that food insecurity can appropriately be addressed by CHES, and more than half indicated that they would be interested in taking part in future research resulting from the current study. Many participants indicated that food insecurity concepts are not being addressed in formal educational programs, and most believed that they should be. The results of the current study indicate that many CHES likely would incorporate information about and strategies to address household food insecurity if they felt they had been adequately trained to do so. Food access issues contribute to negative health and social outcomes and can be seen as negative outcomes themselves; therefore, this increasingly important component of the community and public health workforce should be encouraged and supported in leading efforts to solve these issues. [Author Abstract]

116.) **Penn, D. M.**

Obesity-related comorbidities, disability, physical inactivity, and food insecurity in Georgia senior centers.

Ph.D. dissertation, University of Georgia. 2009.

This dissertation examines the problem of obesity in older adults participating in Georgia's Older Americans Act Nutrition Programs (OAANP) at senior centers. Three studies were conducted that focused on: 1) the influence of obesity on the prevalence of obesity-related comorbidities, 2) the extent to which moderate physical activity attenuated obesity-related comorbidities, and 3) the role of physical limitations as underlying causal factors in the food insecurity-obesity paradox. Obesity markedly increased the prevalence of diabetes, high blood pressure, arthritis, and poor or fair self-reported health by about 20-percentage points. Moderate physical activity did not attenuate the effects of obesity on the comorbidities, but did significantly decrease the risk of poor physical function and poor or fair self-reported health. Obesity and weight-related disability both increased the risk of food insecurity, suggesting that certain physical limitations may contribute to the food insecurity-obesity paradox in older adults. Together these studies demonstrated that obesity markedly increased the risk of several comorbidities and food insecurity, emphasizing the need for health promotion programs at senior centers to promote healthy body weights, nutrition, physical activity, food assistance, and food security. [Author Abstract]

117.) **Peterman, J. L. N.**

Food deprivation, nutrition knowledge, and dietary practices among Cambodian refugee women in Lowell, MA.

Ph.D. dissertation, Tufts University, 2009.

Cambodian refugees in the U.S. have high rates of chronic disease. This may be partially due to trauma and hardship, including lack of food, prior to coming to the U.S. Additionally, the U.S. environment presents Cambodian refugees with highly available and affordable. Most immigrant groups change dietary behaviors with time in the U.S., and many of the changes may lead to increased risk for chronic disease. Dietary practices of Cambodian refugees are not well documented. This thesis collected and analyzed information on past food experiences and current food beliefs, nutrition knowledge, and dietary practices among Cambodian refugee women in Lowell, MA, the second largest Cambodian community in the U.S. Two sets of focus groups were conducted to gather preliminary data on food practices (n=11) and past food experiences (n=11) and to aid in survey development. A survey was developed and administered to 160 women ages 35-60 years old. Prior to coming to the U.S., participants experienced severe food deprivation and food insecurity. Those with higher past food deprivation levels were more likely to report currently eating meat with fat and to be overweight/obese. Acculturation, education, and having attended a nutrition education class were positively related to higher knowledge of the connection between food and health. Higher education, higher acculturation, and having attended a nutrition education class were positively related to some healthful dietary practices. Having a child under 18 years old at home was positively related to some less healthful dietary practices. Past food deprivation combined with availability and affordability of preferred foods in the U.S. may put Cambodian refugees at risk for consumption of less healthful foods and overweight/obesity. Interrupted education has left many older adults at risk for low nutrition knowledge and less healthful dietary practices. Acculturation may provide access to information that encourages more healthful behaviors. Having a child at home may put adults and children at risk for less healthful eating practices. Targeted nutrition education may improve eating practices in this at risk population. Other refugee populations with similar backgrounds may also benefit from this research. [Author Abstract]

118.) **Piaseu, N.**

Food insecurity and health among low income families living in crowded urban areas in Thailand.

Ph.D. dissertation, University of Washington. 2003.

Food insecurity (FI), a situation of an inadequacy in quality and quantity of food, is an increasing public health concern especially in the urban poor. Little is known about how low-income families experience financial crises and FI. The overall objective in this study was to assess perceptions of FI, socioeconomic change, and health among urban poor households in Thailand. This report focuses on 4 operational research questions: (1) what are the socio-economic histories, basic needs, food related behaviors, and perceptions of health that have changed since 1997 among households living in slum areas? (2) what are the experiences of FI in this sample? (3) what social and environmental factors influence FI in these informants? and (4) do descriptions of food security correlate with other indicators of nutritional health measured by dietary intake and anthropometry? A cross-sectional descriptive survey was conducted to identify experiences and influencing factors for FI and health in households living in slum areas. Questionnaires on food security, health, and nutritional assessment, including a 3-day dietary record, and anthropometric measurements were collected from 199 female food providers of households. Overall, households reported lower income, and worse health and life satisfaction as compared to before the economic recession. In addition, a decrease in income led to difficulty meeting their basic needs, such as access to health service and food provision. Results indicated that FI was prevalent. Only 44.2% of the households reported food security whereas 39.2%, 13.6%, and 3% reported FI without hunger, FI with moderate hunger, and FI with severe hunger, respectively. Experiences of FI, and its influencing factors for FI and health, among urban poor families were identified. FI was negatively associated with total calorie intake, nutrient intake, and body weight. Dietary intake and nutrients decreased as FI situations increased. Number of children in household, household income, and support from family predicted FI status among this sample. Improvement in social and health policy for urban poor families is suggested. The results of the study serve as constructive information for developing health programs to empower the urban poor and contribute to health promotion of food security in Thailand. [Author Abstract]

119.) **Putnam, H. R.**

The political ecology of food insecurity in smallholder coffee cooperatives in northern Nicaragua.

Ph.D. dissertation, University of Kansas. 2013.

Food insecurity in smallholder coffee growing communities is recognized as a problem "deserving of a response that reflects its reach" (Caswell 2012, 1). Subject to structural factors including unstable coffee prices, extreme weather shocks, food price swings, smallholder coffee farming households must also access sufficient food and healthy diets amidst an historical trajectory that has incentivized homogenization of available land to coffee cultivation, and restriction of food production, leaving them even more vulnerable to seasonal hunger and chronic malnutrition. Although the relationship between coffee and food insecurity is recognized, its multiscalar dynamics have not been well understood. In this study I investigate and outline the "chain of explanation" (Robbins 2012, 88) of why food insecurity is so persistent in smallholder coffee growing communities. I explore the manifestations of seasonal and chronic hunger, as well as food resilience, which play out in eight first-level cooperatives that are participants in the Youth Leadership and Food Sovereignty Project executed by the cooperative organization the UCA San Ramón, in the department of Matagalpa in northern Nicaragua. Using a combined framework of political ecology, agroecology, and food security and sovereignty, I focus especially on the relationships that contribute to the phenomenon of hunger and insecurity in the eight cooperatives, identifying factors besides overdependence on coffee production on income that contribute to the phenomenon as it manifests in each of the eight cooperatives. My major findings agree with the established understanding that economic dependence on one cash crop (be it coffee or basic grains) leaves farming households unable to provide for themselves during the entire year. I find that more balanced dependence on two or more cash crops is related to longer periods of household provisioning. I also find that finance cycles that farmers must use to purchase seed and food exacerbate the situation. Other factors include the loss of knowledge of seed selection and saving as well as storage infrastructure, loss of healthy food consumption cultures, lack of access to markets for excess production, lack of access to transport and communication infrastructure, and lack of access to water for irrigation and consumption. However, structural factors including a persistent Green Revolution culture, international commodities markets, and contradictory interventions by the state and the coffee industry itself, lead to the conclusion that any set of strategies aiming to relieve seasonal hunger must move beyond price and beyond farm-level interventions to include the participation of actors at all scales. [Author Abstract]

120.) **Quigg, A. M.**

Food insecurity and children's developmental risk: Do anemia and caregiver depression play a role?

Ph.D. dissertation, University of Maryland, Baltimore County. 2010.

Nurturing, sensitive care in early childhood stimulates the developing brain and promotes optimal development, whereas disrupted parenting negatively impacts children's development (Thompson & Nelson, 2001). Food insecurity, caregiver depression, and anemia increase a child's risk for negative developmental outcomes, with chronic experiences having the most negative long-term effects (Campbell & Cohn, 1995; Garmezy, Masten, & Tellegen, 1984; McCann & Ames, 2007; McLoyd, 1998b; NICHD, 2005; Rose-Jacobs, Black, Casey et al., 2008). The current study examined the roles that anemia and maternal depression play in the relation between food insecurity and developmental risk among a low-income, urban, African American sample of young children. This study was part of a larger cross-sectional study of parents with children under age three who seek treatment at pediatric emergency departments or primary care clinics. Participants were approached in waiting rooms and asked if they would like to participate in a survey. Participants who completed surveys in Baltimore's primary care clinic were eligible to be included in the current study if they were a female caregiver and had complete medical record data (i.e., anemia and developmental risk status). Logistic regressions revealed that anemia, defined as hgb < 11 g/dL and hct < 33%, was statistically significantly related to developmental risk (OR = 2.247 [CI: 1.03-

4.902], $p < .05$), suggesting that children with anemia were 2.25 times more likely to be at developmental risk compared to those without anemia. When examined separately, developmental risk, as indicated by the screening instruments (ASQ and DDSTII), was not related to anemia; nor was developmental risk as indicated by the referral and problem list in the medical record. Caregiver report of one or more developmental concerns (OR = 3.372 [95% CI: 1.241-9.166], $p < .05$), and two or more developmental concerns were positively associated with anemia at the hgb<11.0 and hct<33% level (OR = 6.577 [95% CI: 1.559-27.746, $p < .01$). Food insecure caregivers were 2.26 times more likely to report depressive symptoms compared with food secure caregivers (OR = 2.261 [95% CI 1.038-4.924], $p < .05$). These findings highlight both the importance of listening to caregiver's concerns for their children's development and intervening when families experience food insecurity and child anemia. [Author Abstract]

121.) **Ratnayake, M. K.**

Household food insecurity and its implications on health, nutrition and work - a study of a dry land farming community in Sri Lanka.

Ph.D. dissertation, University of London, London School of Hygiene and Tropical Medicine (United Kingdom). 1989.

This thesis describes and discusses a study conducted in a dry land farming community in Southern Sri Lanka between November 1986 and August 1987 with a view to testing the hypothesis that: `Resource poor households with undernourished and sick individuals are constrained by their effective supply of family labour for productive activities. They are thus less efficient, produce less farm output and hence generate little income to acquire food. This puts an extra risk on the more vulnerable households during periods when food availability and the acquirement capacities of households are at their lowest levels'. A selective sample of 66 households was grouped into three social classes, based on household resource ownership patterns. Analysis revealed that although some degree of growth faltering in children is normal occurrence, there was a gradient of severity corresponding to social class. A measurement of current nutritional status appears to be a seasonality in growth patterns of children and energy balance in adults. Although the sample population was of small body size on average, their energy output as a percent of basal metabolic rate appears to be high. Also nutritional status of adult men (BMI), has a positive relationship to the amount of physical work performed in agriculture. However, the observations suggest that those with higher BMI have lower resistance to heat stress during work. The study revealed that by adopting different types of `risk aversion' methods, some households at a relatively high risk were successful in minimising or avoiding ill effects of household food insecurity. Individuals' own perceptions and beliefs, the external social support they received and the methods of risk aversion adopted had a considerable moderating influence on the ill effects of household food availability decline. [Author Abstract]

122.) **Reeder, J. A.**

Harvesting hunger: Measuring food insecurity and hope in Oregon's Mexican agricultural and seafood workers.

Ph.D. dissertation, Oregon State University. 2000.

Food Insecurity exists whenever the availability of nutritionally adequate and safe foods or the ability to acquire acceptable foods in socially acceptable ways is limited or uncertain (EBRO, 1990). Factors that increase a household's risk for food insecurity include being low income and not being able to access formal and informal supplemental food sources. Migrant agricultural workers, defined by the U.S. Department of Labor as persons who travel greater than 75 miles in search of agricultural work, have household incomes less than $10,000 and due to clandestine immigration status or constant relocations may have less access to food assistance programs. Therefore, it is likely that this group is at increased risk for food insecurity. The purpose of this study was to (1) gather demographic information, (2) determine sources of social and emotional support and quantify the amount hope for the future expressed by individuals, and (3) determine what percentage of Oregon's Mexican agricultural workers were food insecure. Subjects (n = 45) were recruited from 3 places of employment representing the seafood processing (3), tree planting (12), and fruit packing industries (30). Some were migrant and seasonal while others had recently settled out of the migrant stream. Participants were either given or read a nine-page Spanish language survey. Thirty-two women and 13 men completed the surveys. The average respondent was 30 years old, married

(45%) or single (36%) and had a household income of less than $15,000 with an average household size of 4.4 persons. Ninety-one percent of participants were born in Mexico. Frequently cited sources of internal support included God (75%), family (70%), myself (45%) and the Church (43%). Sixty-five percent reported having family living close by. Less than one quarter reported finding support in the community. Individual scores on the State Hope scale found that most respondents had a fairly hopeful outlook towards their ability to achieve change. As for food security status, 72.7% were classified as food insecure based on USDA food security module scoring standards. Hope Scale scores were not significantly correlated with food security levels. A lower household income, a larger household size, and fewer years of school were significantly associated with being food insecure. Although a small sample size and departures from traditional methodology make these findings applicable only to the sample populations, it may indicate that food insecurity is a major nutritional risk factor for Mexican agricultural and seafood workers. Validation of the Food Security Module in Spanish is necessary to better determine the prevalence of food insecurity in this population. [Author Abstract]

123.) **Rivera-Marquez, J. A.**

Malnutrition, food insecurity and poverty in older persons from Mexico City.

Ph.D. dissertation, University of London, London School of Hygiene and Tropical Medicine (United Kingdom). 2006.

A theoretical framework has been developed to understand the causal linkages between the determinants of malnutrition, food insecurity and poverty, and current data are then used to describe how this public health concern manifests itself in urban Latin American contexts. This is followed by a discussion of recent social policy, interventions aimed at improving nutrition, access to food and well-being in older people in Latin America. The quantitative part of the thesis presents a study which assessed indicators of nutritional status, food security, health, quality of life and living conditions among 1,263 households with residents aged 70 and over from socio-geographically-defined poor areas of Mexico City and its Metropolitan Zone. The literature suggests that a regular source of economic resources is important to ensure food security during old age; thus the impact of an ongoing old-age monetary-transfer programme on nutrition-related indicators, food security and poverty was assessed at the levels of both older persons and households. This was carried out through a quasi-experimental study using an ex-post comparison of intervention and control groups with no baseline measures. Overall, results suggest differential access to food, quality of life and living conditions according to socioeconomic stratum among older persons and their household contexts. Differences in dietary diversity and food insecurity among older persons were also found, when data were disaggregated by monetary-transfer eligibility status. The old-age intervention analysed in this thesis showed little impact on access to food and other indicators of well-being at household level. There was, however, a high prevalence of people being overweight and obese among the older population under study. Given that this thesis is the first approach to food insecurity ever carried out among urban older populations in Mexico and Latin America, the conclusions emphasise the magnitude of uncertain access to food during old age, and they suggest guidelines for policy makers at different levels of government, stimulating further research on issues related to old age in the region. [Author Abstract]

124.) **Robinson, D. A.**

Perceptions of the food insecure: Does direct authority construct understanding. M.L.A.S. thesis, Western Illinois University. 2012.

Research has shown that the public generally holds a negative perception of those living in poverty, and specifically of those using emergency food assistance programs (Limbert and Bullock 2009). Most of the research has focused on the public perception and political discourse surrounding emergency food assistance recipients; very little research has been devoted to the perspectives of those working directly for food pantries (Duffy et.al 2006; Molnar et.al 2001). This lack of research is problematic considering the power held by those working and volunteering at food pantries. Pantry eligibility and participation can be changed at the discretion of the pantry director. Because of this authority, it is necessary to understand how directors, paid staff, and volunteers view the vulnerable populations that they serve. The purpose of this research project is to get a fuller understanding of how food pantry directors, personnel, and volunteers view the clients served at their pantries, and the larger issues of poverty and assistance programs. Semi-structured interviews were held with both directors and volunteers at various food pantries within both rural and urban settings. These interviews were then analyzed in an attempt to explore how pantry personnel construct their understanding of poverty and food insecurity as larger issues within the communities they serve. The findings of this analysis suggest that pantry personnel were empathetic, most frequently identified systemic causes of poverty, and discussed not only the hardships experienced by their clients, but by the pantries as well. [Author Abstract]

125.) **Rose, L. M.**

Organizing for Social Change: Grassroots Efforts to Reduce Food Insecurity.

Ph.D. dissertation, Ohio University. 2012.

The number of people living in poverty in the United States is the largest it has ever been in the 51 years during which poverty estimates have been published (DeNavas-Walt, Proctor, & Smith, 2010). One area especially plagued with poverty is the Appalachian region of Southeastern Ohio. Despite the existence of government assistance programs, families are experiencing food insecurity and turning to local charitable organizations which are struggling to keep up with demand (see Curry, 2010). In response, a number of organizations have tried to address food insecurity using alternative ways of organizing; this research examines these attempts. It offers unique contributions to health and organizational communication scholarship. I employed interpretive research methods to explore how one community organization, the Community Food Initiatives (CFI), mobilizes people and resources to address food insecurity. Specifically, I engaged in participant-observations, in-depth interviews, and discourse analysis. The constant comparative method was used to identify patterned regularities in the data (e.g., interview transcripts, fieldnotes, and documents). Results offer a description of the systemic and regulatory issues with our current food system, followed by highlighting the ways in which CFI programming mobilizes the community to inspire social change. Next, I discuss the importance of establishing a relationship with your food, arguing for the value of connection to the earth and food systems. Finally, I advance the claim that CFI demands ethical revaluation of caring, work, and community engagement. I close with theoretical and practical implications, limitations, and directions for future research. [Author Abstract]

126.) **Rusness, B. A. R.**

Potential dietary risks and the food insecurity of the homeless.

Ph.D. dissertation, The Fielding Institute. 1990.

Homelessness places individuals at risk for meeting their basic needs of shelter and food. Little research exists on the topic of the food consumption or food insecurity of the homeless. No prior research has evaluated the usual food consumption of homeless individuals over a period of time at the nutrient level. In addition, this work is the first research on the food consumption of the homeless to be grounded in the system's theoretical biopsychosocial model. This study sought (1) to assess a broad range of indicators of food insecurity and specific nutrient deficiencies/excesses in the usual diets of homeless individuals for a past 2-month period according to current recommendations by the National Research Council and (2) to investigate possible relationships between independent demographic, health, and food source factors and dependent dietary risk/food insecurity variables. Homeless adults in Minnesota and North Dakota (N = 560) who utilized services completed a general survey that sought demographic, dietary, and health information. A subgroup of 81 homeless individuals completed the Willett Food Frequency tool for the evaluation of their usual food consumption during the past 2 month period. Interviews with the homeless were conducted to provide a context for understanding the experience and food insecurity of homelessness. The experience of homelessness does place individuals at dietary risk. The homeless had dietary deficiencies in vitamin A, vitamin C, calcium, and iron, along with excesses in total fat consumption. The homeless population had significantly lower intakes of several nutrients than a comparable regional population from the Heart Health study. In addition, the homeless experienced food insecurity in a variety of ways, such as lack of sufficient food, eating less than three meals per day, going without food for a whole day, and worry about food quality/quantity. Certain factors were seen to promote dietary/food insecurity risk. Long-term homelessness, the experience of prior homelessness, non-major usage of shelters as a food source, and poor health (perceived health status of fair/poor and presence of a chronic condition) aggravated the dietary risks inherent in homelessness. [Author Abstract]

127.) **Ryu, J. H.**

Long-Term Patterns of Food Insecurity and Health Status among School-Aged Children.

Ph.D. dissertation, The University of Wisconsin, Madison. 2012.

With sharp increases in the national food insecurity rate over the past several years due to the economic recession, food insecurity has become an issue of public policy as well as public concern. Although past research has demonstrated the associations between food insecurity and a wide array of negative health outcomes in children, little is known about the long-term patterns of food insecurity and the implications of differing patterns of food insecurity for child health outcomes. Using four waves of data from the Early Childhood Longitudinal Study-Kindergarten Cohort 1998-1999 (ECLS-K), this study examines the long-term patterns of food insecurity over multiple years in childhood and the cumulative effects of these patterns on children's health status. This dissertation includes three empirical papers. The first paper describes the long-term dynamics of food insecurity from kindergarten through eighth grade with a focus on examining persistence and severity. Results suggest that food insecurity is generally a transient rather than a persistent condition, and that single-year estimates substantially underestimate the share of children whose households experienced food insecurity at some point during their childhood years. Using logistic regression models, the second paper estimates the cumulative impacts of food insecurity over the observation years on eighth grade health status. Using a summary measure for cumulative exposures to food insecurity over the 9-year period, the analyses demonstrate that persistent food insecurity is associated with lower health status in eighth grade, whereas more transient food insecurity is not significantly associated with health in eighth grade. Moreover, the negative health effect of food insecurity is found in a more moderate level of food insecurity--not just a severe level. The third paper hypothesizes that the biological vulnerability of being born low birthweight would further strengthen the association between food insecurity and changes in health status. However, results show no clear evidence of moderating effects of low birthweight. Findings of this study demonstrate that the detrimental impact of food insecurity, particularly persistent food insecurity, on child health is an important public policy issue. Policy interventions to alleviate children's food insecurity may promote child health and well-being. [Author Abstract]

128.) **Sandmann, L. A.**

An exploratory study of the spatial distribution of Madagascar's deforestation and food insecurity.

M.S. thesis, University of Georgia. 2010.

Although deforestation and food shortages in Madagascar have been thoroughly studied independently, their connections have yet to be investigated. This research aims to explore the relationships between deforestation and food insecurity in Madagascar using a geographic information system (GIS) to model spatial variables related to national land cover, food access, and human health. Based on the United States United States Agency for International Development (USAID) conceptual framework, a new Madagascar Food Insecurity Index (FII) model was created. It contains aspects of social, physical, and biological phenomena that intersect in geographic space to produce insecurity in food access, availability, and utilization. The Madagascar FII model result identified the most food insecure areas as being in the eastern portion of the country. [Author Abstract]

129.) **Sansom, D.**

Vulnerable individuals with diabetes navigating the health care system: A grounded theory study.

Ph.D. dissertation, The University of Nebraska - Lincoln. 2013.

The purpose of this constructivist study was to develop a substantive theory to explain the process of how vulnerable individuals with diabetes who are glycemically controlled navigate the health care system. Grounded theory was the research methodology. The grand tour question guiding the study was: how do vulnerable individuals with diabetes who are glycemically controlled navigate the health care system? For the purposes of the study, vulnerable individuals with diabetes were defined as belonging to at least two of the following groups identified by Shi and Stevens (2010) as vulnerable: predisposing factors (racial/ethnic minorities, elderly), enabling factors (uninsured, low income, unemployed), need factors (depression, chronically ill, disabled veterans). Eighteen of the twenty participants were served by community health centers in an urban setting. Glycemic control for the study was operationally defined as an A1c less than 8% at any time during the last year or "most" capillary blood glucose readings falling under 200 mg/dl. Twenty individuals were recruited into the study using purposive theoretical sampling. Nineteen of the participants were diagnosed with type 2 diabetes mellitus; one participant had type1 diabetes mellitus. Semi-structured interviews were completed and were audio taped. Data analysis was completed using the constant comparative technique. The emerging core category that explained the participants' main problem as well as its solution was Defying Gravity, Through Resilience. The sub-processes identified were: Being Told, Taking Ownership, Well-being as a Protective, Learning about Diabetes, Getting Health Care, Using the Safety Net, Seeking Care, Having Social Supports, Fearing Consequences, Thinking about Diabetes, Wanting to Live, and Facing Struggles. Results of the study have important implications for public health. Although access to care was good for most of the participants, lack of continuity of care, insufficient medical nutritional therapy, and financial/social challenges of food insecurity/ housing hardship were identified as struggles faced by the individuals. The emerging core category, Defying Gravity, Through Resilience, including all sub-processes, explains the participants' ability to achieve glycemic control. [Author Abstract]

130.) **Shanguhyia, N.**

State policy and food insecurity in Kenya's arid and semi-arid land (ASAL) regions. M.A. thesis, West Virginia University. 2008.

Kenya's arid and semi-arid lands (ASALs) have continued to experience chronic and persistent food crises despite the efforts made by governmental and non-governmental organizations to address the problem. Inappropriate policies and poor approaches have partly been blamed for this persistence. This study therefore seeks to examine how food insecurity is conceptualized within policy documents, the perceived causes and solutions, and potential drawbacks of such perceptions. The study adopts a political ecology framework within which Ellis' (2000) rural livelihood approach and Sen's (1981) entitlement thesis are used to analyze selected government policy documents and related reports. A brief historical overview of the political, social and economic history of the ASALs situates the issue in a temporal context and shows how colonial policies set the stage for the marginalization of these regions, a process that has been perpetuated in different ways by subsequent postcolonial regimes. A textual analysis of policy documents reveals contradictions and inconsistencies within and across the documents on key policy issues such as the effects of market liberalization on food security. Furthermore, the spatio-temporal nature of food insecurity in the ASALs poses a unique challenge which has not been adequately addressed by the policies. The findings of this study are relevant to food security and food policy studies, and rural livelihoods and emphasize the need to incorporate contextual differences as well as harmonizing the different policies to effectively address the chronic and persistent food crises in the ASALs. [Author Abstract]

131.) **Sieloff, C. K.**

Food deserts: A feminist study of Washington, D.C.

M.A. thesis, The George Washington University. 2011.

Grocery stores tend to be the main point of purchase for how the majority of Americans attain food. By exploring the location of grocery stores within one city, it is possible to bring to light the gross discrepancy of access to a commodity needed to feed individuals and families. The implications of this access can be traced to a pattern of historical and structural inequality as well as the market forces that hold corporations to meet standard business practices. Any study on food accessibility would be remiss to not explore the impact that accessibility has on women. Recognizing that grocery shopping and most food work is mainly done by women, and that the process of selecting food, creating meals, and doing the tasks that take an item from the store to the table is important from a feminist standpoint. The purpose of this research is to examine access to supermarkets within Washington, D.C. and to determine if access disproportionally impacts women and if this impact is negative. A literature review explores how current studies of food access are conducted, and to determine the concepts used in food access studies. Included is an examination of these studies for their treatment of gender, in addition to race and income. Because I suspect that part of the reason for supermarket location is both structurally and historically motivated, newspaper articles were reviewed covering food access in neighborhoods in Washington, D.C. over the past 50 years. To get a sense of who has access to which supermarkets, demographic data was used, specifically the Census 2000 data by census tract, to examine how the placement of grocery stores could potentially hinder certain groups of people from access to a variety of food options. Finally, policy options were reviewed and offered, as this study indicates that there is an inequitable amount of access to supermarkets and food access within Washington, D.C. [Author Abstract]

132.) **Smith, A. S.**

Exploring food acquisition practices of food-insecure individuals in New Jersey.

Ph.D. dissertation, The Johns Hopkins University. 2010.

The food-insecure confront barriers in obtaining nutritionally adequate and safe foods, in socially acceptable ways. Although this group may struggle to obtain food as a result of financial and environmental obstacles, deaths from starvation in the U.S. are uncommon. In order to maintain an adequate food supply for themselves and their households, individuals resort to employing food acquisition practices that can result in inadequate nutrient intake, consumption of unsafe foods, and engagement in risky and stigmatized behaviors. This research validates an identified compilation of food acquisition practices used by limited-resource individuals in New Jersey, described the users of emergency food providers (EFPs), determined the lifetime and recent prevalence of practices, and compared them to levels of food insecurity. A survey instrument was developed to collect information about sociodemographic influences, modifying conditions, mediating mechanisms, and engagement in the identified practices. After expert review, 10 cognitive interviews were conducted, and the instrument pre-tested with 10 EFP clients. A two-stage random sampling strategy was used, with equal probability of selection of EFPs (n = 50) at the first stage and 10 respondents per site at the second (n = 492). Following site and client consent, trained interviewers conducted semi-structured, in-depth, one-on-one interviews with eligible respondents. Data collection occurred from June 18 to October 31, 2008.

Descriptive analysis using chi-square tests was performed. Bivariate and multivariate logistic regression modeling was performed to elucidate potential confounders. All 78 practices were verified. Nineteen practices had > 50% engagement. Frequency of engagement in most practices increased as food security decreased. The very low food security level had a disproportionately high percentage of monthly household incomes \$1,000 a month (51.5%). Individuals at either end of the study's household monthly income range were significantly more likely to be food-insecure (\$1,000, OR = 1.87). Evidence about the prevalence, extent, and severity of practices used by the food-insecure, and associated influences and mechanisms, can enable policymakers, nutrition educators, food safety experts, and advocates to prioritize and better respond to issues of food insecurity. [Author Abstract]

133.) **Smith, J.**

Food customs of rural and urban Inupiaq elders and their relationships to select nutrition parameters, food insecurity, health, and physical and mental functioning. Ph.D. dissertation, Florida International University. 2007.

The Inupiaq Tribe resides north of the Arctic Circle in northwestern Alaska. The people are characterized by their continued dependence on harvested fish, game and plants, known as a subsistence lifestyle (Lee 2000:35-45). Many are suggesting that they leave their historical home and move to urban communities, places believed to be more comfortable as they age. Tribal Elders disagree and have stated, "Elders need to be near the river where they were raised " (Branch 2005:1). The research questions focused on differences that location had on four groups of variables: nutrition parameters, community support, physical functioning and health. A total of 101 Inupiaq Elders ≥50 years were surveyed: 52 from two rural villages, and 49 in Anchorage. Location did not influence energy intake or intake of protein; levels of nutrition risk and food insecurity; all had similar rates between the two groups. Both rural and urban Elders reported few limitations of ADLs and IADLs. Self-reported general health scores (SF-12.v2 GH) were also similar by location. Differences were found with rural Elders reporting higher physical functioning summary scores (SF-12.v2 PCS), higher mental health scores (SF-12.v2 MH), higher vitality and less pain even though the rural mean ages were five years older than the urban Elders. Traditional food customs appear to support the overall health and well being of the rural Inupiaq Elders as demonstrated by higher intakes of Native foods, stronger food sharing networks and higher family activity scores than did urban Elders. The rural community appeared to foster continued physical activity. It has been said that when Elders are in the rural setting they are near " people they know " and it is a place " where they can get their Native food " (NRC 2005). These factors appear to be important as Inupiaq Elders age, as rural Inupiaq Elders fared as well or better than Inupiaq Elders in terms of diet, mental and physical health. [Author Abstract]

134.) **Smith, J.**

The effect of resource cycling and food insecurity on dietary intake and weight of low-income, single mothers living in rural Louisiana.

M.S. thesis, Louisiana State University. 2002.

Food security, nutritional adequacy, and anthropometrics were assessed in 30 low-income women living in rural Louisiana. For food stamp recipients, a 24-hour-diet recall was collected at the beginning (Day 1) and another at the end (Day 2) of their monthly resource cycle; for non-food stamp recipients, the first 24-hour diet recall was collected at a time that was specified by participants (Day 1) and the second was collected approximately 31/2 weeks later. Twenty-one of the 30 participants received food stamps. Ten of the 30 participants were food insecure. Of the 10 food insecure participants, seven received foods stamps. As a whole, participants were overweight. Irrespective of grouping, participant's diets were similar and poor. Many participants did not consume at least 67% of the Recommended Daily Allowances (RDA) or Dietary Reference Intakes (DRI) for energy; calcium; iron; zinc; folate; and vitamins A, D, E, and C. Participants were more likely to meet at least 67% of the RDA or DRI for protein; vitamins B6 and B12; niacin; thiamin; and riboflavin. With the exception of the fats/sweets group, participants also failed in meeting the Food Guide Pyramid recommendations. Between 30% and 50% of the entire population exceeded the National Cholesterol Education Program recommendations for total fat, saturated fat, and cholesterol. The number of eating episodes and number of different foods consumed was also low. Food insecure participants had a significantly higher weight (p=0.0079), body mass index (p=0.0135), and percent body fat (p=0.0298) than food secure participants. A significant difference was found between Day 1 and Day 2 for mean differences in energy (p=0.0367), saturated fat (p=0.0178), and monounsaturated fat (p=0.0324) for food stamp recipients and non food stamp recipients. There was a significant difference between Day 1 and Day 2 in the mean number of servings of fats and sweets consumed for the entire population (p=0.0183). Participants were unable to define a "balanced meal." Inadequate nutrient intake increases the risk of developing a nutrition-related disease. Nutrition education programs could benefit participants in making better food choices [Author Abstract]

135.) **Solorio, C. M. G.**

Maternal Food Insecurity, Child Feeding Practices, Weight Perceptions and BMI in a Rural, Mexican-Origin Population.

M.S. thesis, University of California, Davis. 2013.

Among Mexican-American children, 35-40% are overweight. To achieve the Healthy People 2020 goal of reducing childhood obesity, interventions must be developed based on an understanding of the origins of childhood obesity. The goal of this study was to determine relationships between maternal food insecurity, child feeding practices and perceived child weight in a Mexican-origin population. Data were obtained through food security and medical history surveys along with anthropometric measurements of 175 Mexican-origin mother-child dyads living in rural, agricultural towns. No relationships were seen between food insecurity and other variables; however, only 31% of mothers of overweight children accurately identified them as such and only 47% of these mothers reported an attempt to change her child's nutrition or physical activity. This study exposed the need to determine factors involved in the identification of childhood obesity and in how mothers decide to change nutrition and physical activity for their children. [Author Abstract]

136.) **Stephen, L. J.**

Vulnerability and food insecurity in Ethiopia: forging the links between global policies, national strategies and local socio-spatial analyses. (BL: DN063460).

D.Phil. dissertation, University of Oxford (United Kingdom). 2003.

In this thesis it is argued that social processes, inherent in the structure of societies and institutions, combine globally, nationally and locally to undermine the treatment of vulnerability to food insecurity as a variable, place-based phenomenon. The arguments are developed with reference to food policy and vulnerability assessments in Ethiopia during the 1990s. Specific references are made to the findings from interviews with national early warning system staffs carried out in 1997 and 1998 and to food security surveys in Delanta Dawint, Ethiopia carried out in 1998. The research and discussion concentrates on events in Ethiopia during the 1990s, with reflections on important antecedents dating from 1972. The 1970s to 1990s saw dramatic political transitions: from an imperial government to a centralized command economy based on the socialist model, to a decentralized democratically orientated government and sub-national regional restructuring. Struggles for political independence and human rights also distinguish these decades. One of the aims of rebel movements in the 1970s, for example, was to remove power from the ruling monarchy, and from the Amhara ethnic group who were perceived to have benefited from sharing the same ethnicity as the monarchy. Land tenure arrangements under the monarchy followed traditional rules. However, under the subsequent socialist system customary rights were dissolved and land was appropriated for government purposes. In the 1990s, under the new Democratic Republic of Ethiopia a new form of land allocation emerged as geographical regions were established according to ethnic composition. Despite the differences in the aims of each government administration, aspects of policies under each regime have augmented the divide between national and local and have increased the sense of insecurity amongst rural people. This has contributed to their vulnerability. [Author Abstract]

137.) **Stormer, A.**

The relationship between food insecurity and cognitive and social skills of kindergartners in the United States.

Ph.D. dissertation, Tulane University. 2003.

The development in the last decade of methodology for measuring and scaling household food insecurity and hunger in U.S. populations makes systematic examination of the ways in which hunger and food insecurity affect individuals and families possible. The impact of food insecurity on children has always been of primary concern for policy, advocacy, and science because of the vulnerability of children to long-term developmental sequelae. There is an emerging and rapidly growing literature demonstrating deleterious links between inadequate food and a variety of developmental outcomes for children, including poorer health status, school absenteeism, and emotional and behavioral dysfunction. The research presented here explores the relationship of household food insecurity to children's well-being in terms of cognitive and social development at kindergarten entry, utilizing a large and representative sample children in the United States. The timing of this evaluation, in the fall and spring of the child's first school experience, allows not only a snapshot of a child's development throughout his/her preschool years but also the effect of the first year of schooling in relation to these outcomes. The data are from the Early Childhood Longitudinal Study of Kindergartners (ECLS-K), collected in 1998-99 by the National Center for Education Statistics, and comprise 20,929 children attending 1,000 private and public schools. Results indicate that measures of reading, math, and general knowledge competence were not impacted by household food insecurity independent of other influences, but child emotional and functioning were negatively associated with household food insecurity even when controlling for many other relevant variables. The relationship of household food insecurity to children's attained growth was also examined and no independent relationship of household food insecurity to height for age or weight for height was found in either the fall or the spring of kindergarten. [Author Abstract]

138.) **Tawodzera, G.**

Vulnerability and resilience in crisis: urban household food insecurity in Harare, Zimbabwe.

Ph.D. dissertation, University of Cape Town (South Africa). 2010.

Includes bibliographical references (leaves 191-222). Within the context of demographic growth, rapid urbanization and rising urban poverty which characterizes much of Sub-Saharan Africa in the 21st Century, this thesis examines the urban poors vulnerability to food insecurity and analyses the strategies that households adopt to enhance their resilience in this challenging environment. Harare is the study site, providing an acute example of a city (and country) in crisis, and a context in which formal food markets have failed to meet the needs of the urban poor, within a generalized collapse of the economy. The central question, then, is how do the urban poor meet their food needs under such conditions of extreme material deprivation?; Includes abstract. [Author Abstract]

139.) **Tayie, F. A. K.**

Associations between adult food insecurity and various nutritional outcomes.

Ph.D. dissertation, Auburn University. 2008.

The purpose of this dissertation is to provide a better understanding of the health and nutritional status of food insecure persons in the United States. This dissertation covers three studies which used data from the National Health and Nutrition Examination Surveys 1999-2002. The first study determined the associations between adult food insecurity and percent body fat (%BF), BMI and height, and %BF and BMI stratified by height. Bioelectrical impedance analysis was used to determine percent body fat for 2,117 men and 1,909 women. Results showed that, among men, %BF, height and BMI decreased as food insecurity (FI) increased. Marginal food security among women who were below median height associated with about 2.0 kg/m 2 increase in BMI compared with their fully food secure counterparts, P = 0.042. Marginal food security among women associated with 1.3 cm decrease in height, P = 0.016. Percent body fat did not associate with food insecurity among women irrespective of height. The second study determined the associations between adult food insecurity and body weight change among 2,626 men and 2,685 women in 1 and 10 years using different specifications. Results showed that compared with the fully food secure, food insecurity among women associated with significant weight gain at both the >5kg and >10kg specifications in both 1 and 10 years. Food insecurity associated with higher prevalence of weight gain ≥ 10% of body weight 1 year ago among women and 10 years ago among men. Food insecurity without hunger among women associated with greater likelihood to gain >5kg of weight in 1 year. The third study estimated the probabilities of dyslipidemia and elevated plasma glucose (EPG) in relation to food insecurity among 2,572 men and 2,976 women. Results showed that, compared with the fully food secure, significantly higher percentage of marginally food secure women and food insecure without hunger women associated with dyslipidemia. Marginally food security and food insecurity without or with hunger among women associated with dyslipidemia. It was concluded that, among men, food insecurity without and with hunger associate with decreases in height, percent body fat and BMI. Among women, intermediate-level food insecurity associates with increased BMI, decreased height, greater weight gain and dyslipidemia. These results highlight the need to re-invigorate public health efforts towards improvement of food security and alleviate its effects both in the short and long term in the United States. [Author Abstract]

140.) **Taylor, L. O.**

The relationship between food security status and dietary intake and weight fluctuations within individuals with serious mental illness.

M.S. thesis, University of Kansas. 2011.

Food insecurity is a serious health issue that can lead to many health consequences, including poor nutritional intake and obesity. Individuals with serious mental illness may be susceptible to food insecurity and the accompanying health consequences. The purpose of this study was to determine the effects of food insecurity on nutritional intake and to determine if food insecure individuals with serious mental illness experience a cyclic overconsumption pattern that leads to weight gain. Twenty-two individuals with serious mental illness, 9 of whom were food insecure and 13 of whom were food secure, completed the 8-week study. All subjects completed the U.S. Household Food Security Questionnaire to determine food security status. Weight was measured weekly, and dietary recalls were taken at the beginning and end of each month (at weeks 1, 4, 5, and 8). The healthy eating index (HEI) was used to determine diet quality. All dietary recalls were entered into NDSR and HEI, and energy intake was determined at each time point. A general mixed modeling analysis that accounts for dependence among observations was used for analysis. A significant decrease in weight over time was found as well as a significant decrease in energy intake from the beginning of the month to the end of the month in both the food secure and food insecure groups. There was no significant difference in HEI and macronutrient consumption across the month. There was also no significant difference between groups in weight, energy intake, HEI, or macronutrient consumption. Both the food secure and food insecure groups scored lower than the average American's HEI score of 58.2 at both the beginning and end of the month. These findings suggest that all individuals with serious mental illness may have trouble acquiring and keeping a constant and nutritionally adequate food supply throughout the month and may benefit from classes teaching them how to grocery shop for low cost nutritional foods, how to better budget money, how to maintain their food supply, and how to cook with the foods that they do have as well as simple cooking methods. [Author Abstract]

141.) **Ten Haagen, K. S.**

Relationship among housing quality, food insecurity, social service needs, domestic violence, and mental health needs of children and families.

Ph.D. dissertation, The University of North Carolina, Chapel Hill. 2013.

This study examined the predictive quality of housing problems, food insecurity, social service needs and various demographic co-variates in determining the presence or absence of domestic violence problems and mental health needs. The study utilized secondary data for a group of participants including 308female parent/guardians recruited over a 12-month period from the Children's Hospital Primary Care Center (CHPCC) at Children's Hospital Boston. Families attending the health center that completed the survey were primarily from low-income and predominantly Hispanic and African American. A series of logistic regression models found a marginally significant effect for the relationship between housing problems and domestic violence problems, and a significant effect for the relationship between social service need and domestic violence problems. No relationship was found between all predictor variables and reports of mental health need. Implications for research and practice are considered. [Author Abstract]

142.) **Tong, Z.**

Poverty, food insecurity and commercialization in rural China.

Ph.D. dissertation, University of Guelph (Canada). 1994.

This study analyzes the relationship among poverty, food insecurity, and commercialization in rural China by employing agricultural household models. Data are derived from a 10,000 household subsample of the annual rural household consumption and expenditure survey. In general, rural China appears to have no serious food insecurity issue, primarily because land is equally distributed. Groups which are identified as "food insecure" from sample data are not poor in income, and behave more as if they have strong preferences for producing and/or consuming commodities other than food. The results of econometric models of rural household supply and demand for staple food show that both own-price and cross-price elasticities of marketed surplus of grains are high, and in both affluent and poor areas. However, among low income groups, the profit effect is sufficient to turn the own-price elasticity negative. Overall increases in market prices of food should result in significant increases in marketed surplus. However, government only controls quota amounts and prices, and if it promotes commercialization by increasing quota prices or eliminating quota procurement requirements, marketed surplus is likely to decline sharply. The fundamental difference between poor and non-poor areas is found, not in commercial or consumer behaviour, but in productivity. Improvement of rural infrastructure and assistance in developing more advanced technology would be the most critical parts of a poverty alleviation strategy. [Author Abstract]

143.) **Tonn, N. A.**

Food Insecurity and Self-Reported Psycho-Social Health Status in Manitoba First Nation Communities: Results from the Manitoba First Nations Regional Longitudinal Health Survey 2002/2003.

M.Sc. thesis, University of Manitoba (Canada). 2012.

The purpose of the study is to provide a descriptive analysis of food insecurity within the adult First Nations population in Manitoba. A bivariate analysis is used to determine strength of relationships between food insecurity and socio-demographic variables as well as self-reported general health and psycho-social health. This research study also includes a gender-based analysis (GBA), which allows for possible food insecurity prevalence differences between women and men. The data obtained for this research study is from the second wave of the Manitoba First Nations Regional Longitudinal Health Survey (MFNRLHS, 2002/2003). Select socio-demographic variables as well as self-reported general health status, 'life balance,' and elements of psycho-social health, including self-reported health, 'life balance,' depression, intense anxiety, stress level, and domestic dispute were included. A P-value of 0.05 was used to identify significant differences. Significant results from this study include elevated food insecurity in Manitoba First Nations (37.2%). The bivariate analysis reveals that food insecurity is marginally associated with age group, with the highest food insecurity among young and middle-aged women; middle-aged men, and those with lone-parent status. Food insecurity is also significantly associated with total household income, the number of incomes per household, as well as employment versus government support over a two-year period. Food insecurity is elevated in both southern (29.4%) and northern (51.4%) regions of the province. [Author Abstract]

144.) **Towers, K. M.**

To have and have not: Household determinants of food insecurity by age in a sample of Iowa food pantry recipients.

M.S. thesis, Iowa State University. 2009.

As the United States population ages and their healthcare needs grow it is necessary to examine health-related issues experienced by this population. Food insecurity is one such issue impacting not only older adults but the general population as well. Working to better understand determinants of food insecurity and what factors may protect against it may help in the fight against it. Cross-sectional data from a survey studying food pantry clients living in four Iowa counties were used to (1) explore what household characteristics may increase the likelihood of experiencing food insecurity and (2) identify what resources may protect against it. The sample was divided into two age groups, those younger than age sixty and those age sixty and older, allowing for a deeper understanding of how food security may differ between age groups. Binary logistic regression was performed to assess the relationship between the dependent variable, household food security status, and multiple independent variables including health status, income, home ownership, employment, employment of household members, Supplemental Nutrition Assistance Program (SNAP) participation, housing assistance participation, and food pantry clients. Control variables included in the regression analysis were total number of household members, and the age, gender, and education of the respondent. Hypotheses were partially confirmed. Independent variables significantly related to the household's food security status included the health status of the respondent, household income, SNAP participation, food pantry participation, receiving housing assistance, and the gender and age of the respondent. Respondent health status was the only independent variable significant for both age groups potentially indicating the costs of meeting one's health care needs may impact meeting the household's food needs regardless of the age of the household head (i.e., the survey respondent). It should be noted that it is possible that other relationships between the independent variables and food security existed; however, they occurred to such a small degree that they were not captured in the regression results. Despite limitations such as the sample being drawn through convenience sampling and generally lacking representativeness, these findings do offer guidance for future research. [Author Abstract]

145.) **Townsend, M. S.**

The relationships of income and food insecurity with overweight in women.

Ph.D. dissertation, The Pennsylvania State University. 2000.

Problem: Obesity is a health problem in the US and its prevalence is increasing. There was a 32% increase in the rate of overweight from 1980 to 1994 when 33% of adults were identified as having BMI's over the cut point. Obesity is not randomly distributed through the population. The prevalence is greatest among low socioeconomic status groups. Despite the research, scientists still do not know why this is so. While the prevalence of obesity is increasing, food insecurity is also increasing. It is assumed that authentic food insecurity is only found among the underweight. An estimated 30 million Americans experience food insecurity making it a concern to nutritionists, legislators and other policy makers. Objectives. The two main purposes of this dissertation research are to examine the inverse relationship of income and overweight to determine why low-income groups have a higher rate of overweight and to determine if food insecurity is related to overweight. Methods: Analyses were performed using the Continuing Survey of Intakes by Individuals (n = 4537) and the Diet and Health Knowledge Survey (n = 2720) for years 1994-1996 and included Chi Square, ANOVA (general linear model) and logistic regression. Twenty variables were defined and compiled using psychosocial. theories and Social Learning Theory. Results: From the 450 articles reviewed for this research, 42 variables were identified that have a relationship with obesity. Of those, a small subset was shown to be related to income and or socioeconomic status (SES).

Twenty of these variables are part of the analyses in this dissertation. In this dataset, Education is a more important socioeconomic variable than income in explaining the inverse relationship between SES and body weight status. In the final model, 94% of income's effect on overweight is explained by education, ethnicity, age, perceived control of body weight, TV viewing, smoking and alcohol while income is non-significant. In another analysis, overweight was found among the food insecure. The prevalence is higher among the food insecure than the food secure. Overweight is an unexpected health outcome of food insecurity. Both the negative SES/overweight and the positive food insecurity/overweight relationships were found among women. Similar relationships were not found among men. These results should be considered exploratory. Discussion: Because of the large number of variables involved, fully understanding why low-income groups have more obesity than other groups may take years of additional research. This research would involve improved quality of existing items on national surveys and testing of variables for reliability (stability) and criterion validity. Researchers should include education as a surrogate for socioeconomic status in models studying the SES/overweight relationship. In addition, this research provides the initial step in documenting the existence of a relationship between food insecurity and overweight using a nationally representative sample of the US population. Further research to confirm these findings is recommended. Given that both the rates of obesity and food insecurity are on the rise, this is an important topic for further investigation. There are public policy implications for many of USDA's food assistance and education programs. Elaboration of both relationships, food insecurity/obesity and SES/obesity, will allow for better intervention designs and evaluations. The fact that food insecurity has unexpected and paradoxical consequences--higher obesity rates and the potential for increased incidence of obesity-related chronic diseases--needs to be addressed. [Author Abstract]

146.) **Travis, A.**

The Supplemental Nutrition Assistance Program and Adherence to Nutritional Guidelines for Fruit and Vegetable Consumption.

Ph.D. dissertation, Walden University. 2012.

The U.S. economic downturn, which began in 2007, has caused soaring unemployment rates, placing many people at risk for mental and physical health problems. The Supplemental Nutrition Assistance Program (SNAP) is a federal entitlement program provided to qualifying low-income families and individuals to improve food purchasing power and prevent food insecurity and malnutrition. Previous research has indicated that the effect of SNAP on health, well-being, and diet quality is controversial, and that a significant portion of female SNAP participants do not adhere to national guidelines for fruit and vegetable consumption. The goal of this study was to use grounded theory to understand female SNAP participants' thoughts, attitudes, and perceptions about how the program influences diet quality. Data were collected during 4 focus groups followed by inductive qualitative analysis. A convenience sample of 21 female adult SNAP participants who met the income eligibility criteria was employed. The results indicated that participants had positive attitudes towards fruits and vegetables. Personal choices affected diet quality, but perishability, transportation, and competing expenses limited diet quality. Participants communicated feelings of hardship, due to uncertainty surrounding the benefit and perceived inadequacy of the allowance. Participants' suggestions for improvement presented in this study constitute an important contribution to the existing literature and may enhance social change initiatives by providing information to key stakeholders. These individuals and groups can use the information to produce evidence-based programs, interventions, and policies, or to provide additional assistance to improve adherence to dietary guidelines and diet quality. [Author Abstract]

147.) **Tuttle, C.**

Household Decisions Related to Food Access and Expenditure: Essays on Food Insecurity and SNAP Participation in the United States.

Ph.D. dissertation, University of Minnesota. 2013.

Recent trends in food insecurity and participation in the Supplemental Nutrition Assistance Program have highlighted the need to re-examine the effectiveness of the current SNAP as well as overlooked predictors of food insecurity. In Essay 1, this dissertation estimates the effect of the implementation of the American Recovery and Reinvestment Act on food expenditure of SNAP participants and finds increases in benefit levels resulted in higher levels of food expenditure above and beyond the effect on total expenditure. Essay 2 examines the effects of energy price shocks on the probability of varying levels of food insufficiency and finds unexpected energy price shocks significantly affect the probability of each food insufficiency indicator. Finally, Essay 3 examines the relationship between time spent in food-related activities and food insecurity and SNAP participation and finds significant relationships between food preparation and food insecurity as well as eating and SNAP participation. [Author Abstract]

148.) **van den Boogaard, R.**

Food insecurity and entitlements among Turkana pastoralists, Northern Kenya. Ph.D. dissertation, University of Sussex (United Kingdom). 2003.

This study focuses on the linkage between environment, livestock production, assets and market exchanges in the analysis of food insecurity of pastoralists in Turkana District, Kenya. Turkana is an arid to semi arid district, with highly variable rainfall and production levels, and recurrent periods of food insecurity. The research examines levels of environmental and livestock production, linkages to the pastoral economy and levels of food security. It also looks at customary and institutional responses to food insecurity. This is done using a variety of methods, mostly derived from the entitlement theory. A major source for this research comes from data collected by the Turkana Drought Contingency Planning unit between 1988 and 1994, although several other sources were also used. In protecting entitlements, Turkana pastoralists have developed significant customary practices of herd management and nutrition. However, these practices have not prevented high levels of food insecurity, mostly as a result of drought. Responses by government and donors have thus far only had marginal results in the protection of entitlements. The study confirms the interaction and linkages between the processes of environmental and livestock production as well as market exchanges and the impact on food security, but there is also evidence that ill-designed economic policies may contribute drastically to increasing levels of food insecurity. The high variability of the ecosystem, causes highly variable production rates which in turn have an impact on markets and food security. A main conclusion is the existence of a timelag between the decline of production and the drastic decline of entitlements. The study confirms the possibility of entitlement protection by utilising early mitigation interventions during situations of food insecurity. Thus far, only food aid distribution has received attention on large scale. [Author Abstract]

149.) **Venci, B. J.**

Functional limitation and chronic diseases are associated with food insecurity among U.S. adults: National Health Interview Survey, 2011.

M.S. thesis, University of Cincinnati. 2013.

Certain chronic diseases are more prevalent in food insecure populations than food secure populations. Little research has examined the association of functional limitation with food insecurity. We examined associations of functional limitation due to any health problems and six chronic diseases (arthritis, diabetes, coronary heart disease, heart attack, hypertension, and stroke) with food security. We conducted secondary analyses using the 2011 National Health Interview Survey for 30,010 adults (≥ 18 y). Adults were categorized into food secure, low food secure or very low food secure. We used multivariate logistic regressions to estimate adjusted odds ratio (aOR) and 95% CI for having functional limitation and chronic disease in low food secure or very low food secure compared to food secure group, while adjusting for sociodemographic and lifestyle factors. The prevalence of functional limitation and the chronic diseases were higher in low food secure and very low food secure than food secure adults. The aORs (95% CIs) for functional limitation were 1.87 (1.63, 2.14) in low food secure and 2.19 (1.91, 2.52) in very low food secure. The range of aORs (95% CIs) were from 1.26 (1.06, 1.51) for diabetes to 1.51 (1.12, 2.04) for stroke in low food secure, and from 1.23 (1.02, 1.48) for diabetes to 1.75 (1.37, 2.24) for coronary heart disease in the very low food secure compared to food secure adults. Our findings indicate that food insecurity is associated with functional limitation and chronic diseases, while directionality is unknown. Interventions for the food insecure populations should address not only food accessibility but also a healthy lifestyle to reduce chronic diseases and functional limitation. [Author Abstract]

150.) **Villanova, C.**

The Relationship between Food Insecurity and Weight Status, Eating Behaviors, the Home Food Environment, Meal Planning and Preparation, and Perceived Stress in Parents Living in the Phoenix Metropolitan Area.

M.S. thesis, Arizona State University. 2014.

Objectives: Through a cross-sectional observational study, this thesis evaluates the relationship between food insecurity and weight status, eating behaviors, the home food environment, meal planning and preparation, and perceived stress as it relates to predominantly Hispanic/Latino parents in Phoenix, Arizona. The purpose of this study was to address gaps in the literature by examining differences in "healthy" and "unhealthy" eating behaviors, foods available in the home, how time and low energy impact meal preparation, and the level of stress between food security groups. Methods Parents, 18 years or older, were recruited during two pre-scheduled health fairs, from English as a second language classes, or from the Women, Infants, and Children's clinic at a local community center, Golden Gate Community Center, in Phoenix, Arizona. An interview, electronic, or paper survey were offered in either Spanish or English to collect data on the variables described above. In addition to the survey, height and weight were collected for all participants to determine BMI and weight status. One hundred and sixty participants were recruited. Multivariate linear and logistic regression models, adjusting for weight status, education, race/ethnicity, income level, and years residing in the U.S., were used to assess the relationship between food security status and weight status, eating behaviors, the home food environment, meal planning and preparation, and perceived stress. Results: Results concluded that food insecurity was more prevalent among parents reporting lower income levels compared to higher income levels (p=0.017). In adjusted models, higher perceived cost of fruits (p=0.004) and higher perceived level of stress (p=0.001) were associated with food insecurity. Given that the sample population was predominately women, a post-hoc analysis was completed on women only. In addition to the two significant results noted in the adjusted analyses, the women-only analysis revealed that food insecure mothers reported lower amounts of vegetables served with meals (p=0.019) and higher use of fast-food when tired or running late (p=0.043), compared to food secure mothers. Conclusion Additional studies are needed to further assess differences in stress levels between food insecure parents and food insecure parents, with special consideration for directionality and its relationship to weight status. [Author Abstract]

151.) **Waity, J. F.**

Is there a persistent rural-urban divide? Spatial inequalities in food insecurity and the impact of the Great Recession.

Ph.D. dissertation, Indiana University. 2013.

In this analysis, I examine the boundaries between rural and urban America using the case of food insecurity, an important indicator of material deprivation. I assess spatial inequalities using a multi-method comparative design that centers on differences in food security and food assistance usage in rural and urban areas, and I include a longitudinal component to assess the impact of the Great Recession on spatial inequalities in food security. Results from the statistical analysis of nationally-representative survey data indicate relatively few spatial inequalities in food security, with rural residents being more food secure only in certain years. While rural residents are more likely to use SNAP, their reliance on food pantries and soup kitchens is no different from urban residents. The effect of the Great Recession was to increase food insecurity and utilization of all assistance programs, with no differential impact on rural and urban areas. Findings from Geographic Information Systems analysis of urban and rural counties in Indiana suggest that differential access to these community-based forms of assistance contributes to the persistence of a rural-urban divide, with rural high-poverty counties having the least access to food assistance. Interview data collected from directors of food assistance programs in Indiana indicate more similarities than differences. These agencies have similar barriers to access despite level of rurality. In general, these food assistance programs are increasingly formalized, bureaucratized, integrated and essential components of hunger relief in the U.S. These findings are consistent with the thesis of a disappearing rural-urban divide, but they also represent a crisis in the U.S. safety net. Overall, this research underscores the need for the expansion of the SNAP program as the key policy instrument to minimize or eliminate spatial inequalities in food insecurity in conjunction with more community-based assistance available to those who currently lack access. [Author Abstract]

152.) **Warshawsky, D. N.**

State, civil society, and food insecurity in post-Apartheid Johannesburg.

Ph.D. dissertation, University of Southern California. 2011.

In contrast to the burgeoning research field on South African civil society, little research has been conducted on the South African food security sector, particularly in urban areas. This is especially pressing given that urban food insecurity continues to persist in South African cities and NGO and CBOs have grown to become important players in the South African urban fabric. To fill this gap, this dissertation focuses on the role of civil society organizations in the food security sector in Johannesburg. In particular, this dissertation focuses on two main research goals. First, this study identifies the institutional roles that the South African state, civil society, and private sector play in procuring food security in Johannesburg. Although it is well-known that each sector of South African society provides food security services in some capacity, little research has been completed which actually delineates the size, scope, and geography of the food security sector in Johannesburg.Second, this research delineates the key processes transforming the South African state's relationship with food security and hunger focused NGOs and CBOs in Johannesburg, including increased governmental and private sector presence in service provisioning, profound resources crisis for civil society organizations, and introduction of American food banking models into South Africa, in the form of FoodBank South Africa and its local subsidiary, FoodBank Johannesburg. It is expected that these key processes have transformed the food security sector in

Johannesburg since the fall of Apartheid in 1994; yet, it is unknown how, if at all, these powerful forces have affected food security organizations in Johannesburg. To achieve these research goals, multiple methods are used including surveys, in-depth interviews, seven month participant observation, quantitative data analysis, and GIS-based spatial analysis. Findings indicate that three global, regional, and local processes have combined to transform the South African state's relationship with food security focused NGOs (non-governmental organizations) and CBOs (community based organizations) in post-Apartheid Johannesburg. These three multi-scalar processes include the financial and human resource crisis among post-Apartheid civil society, reemergence of the South African central state in food security programming, and introduction of American food banking models into South Africa.

First, data analysis reveals that resources in the food security sector are unevenly available by geographic location. While survey data reveal that more organizations are located in inner city locations, wealthier White, suburban locations tend to have much larger, privately resourced organizations. In contrast, Black, inner city locations tend to have a mix of NGOs and CBOs with medium-sized budgets resourced from the private sector and other funding, not government funding. Also, Black, informal settlement and township locations tend to have smaller, governmentally resourced organizations with higher turnover rates. Moreover, there are significant gaps in human resource availability, as organizations in non-suburban areas often have few to no paid staff or volunteers. Second, the reconsolidation of South African central state power has shaped civil society's access to funding, program priorities, and relations with government. This has been exacerbated by the central state's uncoordinated approach to food security policy, lack of attention to urban food security, and disconnectedness from ―on the ground realities.‖ Third, the globalization of the American food banking model into South Africa has transformed NGOs and CBOs through processes of inclusion and exclusion and legitimized a top-down approach towards food security which privileges particular food security interventions over others. While FoodBank Johannesburg has streamlined food donation processes, increased the amount of food delivered, and reduced waste, it has the potential to depoliticize hunger, create new bureaucracies, and allow government to shirk responsibilities towards the food insecure. In addition, the underdevelopment of ―right to food‖ social movements in Johannesburg has limited the politicization of NGO and CBO service delivery and therefore minimized the potential for more progressive state policies to develop in South Africa. Even though South Africa has one of the most politically active civil societies in the world, no substantial food security and hunger focused social movements currently exist in Johannesburg due to limited financial and human resource capacity, lack of a consistent political rallying point, and focus on building social service structures. While some scholars of urban development conceptualize the South African state-civil society problematic as one of limited civil society autonomy, others theorize these new relationships as an explicit co-optation of civil society organizations by the state and part of a broader political agenda to limit their activism and restrict their role to social service delivery. According to this latter approach, civil society inclusive of NGOs, CBOs, and social movements is assumed to work in opposition to the state, and hence the state's need to curtail its autonomy. In the case of the food security sector in Johannesburg, I contend that civil society is not simply opposed to the central state; the landscape of relationships is far more complex, and includes NGOs working in collaboration with capital as well as CBOs and social movements that operate independently of capital or state partnerships. For some NGOs, institutional stability has been ensured by changing organizational mission, accessing private sector funding, or joining forces with FoodBank Johannesburg. Yet, for many NGOs and CBOs, resource unavailability, ineffective governmental policy, and new food bank bureaucracies portend an uncertain future. [Author Abstract]

153.) **Watson, K. B.**

Cross-cultural equivalence and associations among food insecurity and parental influences of children's fruit and vegetable consumption.

Ph.D. dissertation, The University of Texas School of Public Health. 2009.

Over the past several decades, the prevalence of obesity has dramatically increased. Cause for concern has increased because overweight and obesity are major contributors to morbidity and mortality. Intervention research aimed at reducing the prevalence of obesity has identified the family, specifically the parent, as a key component of the home environment. However, findings from dietary behavior change interventions have been disheartening because few studies have reported meaningful change, suggesting methodological and/or measurement issues within the intervention process. A lack of appropriate mediators and cross-cultural equivalence may partially explain the reason for little change. The study aims were to (1) evaluate the psychometric properties and assess the cross cultural equivalence of the Food Insecurity Scale (paper 1) and the modified Parent Feeding Practices Questionnaire (paper 2) and to assess the overall relationships among food insecurity, parent mediators, and parent behaviors towards children's dietary behavior (paper 3) through structural equation modeling and tests of invariance. The study aims were accomplished through conducting secondary analyses using baseline data from English- and Spanish-speaking Hispanic women who participated in the Healthy Families: Step by Step (BHF) study. Results indicated that although the FIS and the mPFPQ exhibited sound psychometric properties, the instruments exhibited a lack of invariance across language spoken groups. The lack of invariance was more pronounced in the FIS. Results also supported the theoretical framework identifying parent's perceived barriers and self-efficacy as mediators of parent's behaviors toward improving children's health eating. Results did not suggest that the relationships were moderated by food insecurity. In conclusion, the identification of differential item functioning in food insecurity and parent feeding practices may be beneficial in enhancing tailored interventions through the incorporation of cultural differences into the change mechanisms. However, future research needs to be conducted to determine if the lack of invariance demonstrates the existence of item bias or if it is a reflection of true difference among the language spoken groups. Additionally, obesity intervention studies targeting parent/family barriers and parent self-efficacy to provide/encourage healthy diets may result in an increase in parent behaviors which promote healthy eating behaviors among children. Future research should also examine a more complete causal pathway to determine whether parental changes in the mediators ultimately lead to an increase in healthy dietary behavior among children. [Author Abstract]

154.) **Webber, M.**

Relationship between food insecurity and overweight in preschool-aged children in rural West Virginia.

M.S. thesis, West Virginia University. 2007.

The prevalence of overweight among adults and children continues to increase. The purpose of this study was to evaluate demographic factors that may be associated with an increase in a child's weight status. Subjects were children aged 2 to 6 years old in two southern West Virginia counties, McDowell and Mercer. Children were weighed and measured, and BMI was calculated. Parents or other caregivers were asked to complete a questionnaire regarding child's age, household food security, and parents' age, height and weight, education level, and hours worked per week. A positive association between food insecurity and overweight among children was present ($p=0.06$). The mother's BMI was positively associated with the child's BMI ($p<0.05$), however the father's BMI was positively associated with only the girl's BMI ($p=0.02$). The only significant association with the parents' education was that dad's educational attainment was associated with an increase in boys' BMI. This study revealed important information regarding relationships between household demographics and overweight in children. [Author Abstract]

155.) **Wetherill, M. S.**

Food insecurity among low-income HIV-positive Oklahomans: Prevalence, determinants, and impact.

Ph.D. dissertation, The University of Oklahoma Health Sciences Center. 2013.

Food insecurity and perceived HIV stigma have been identified as possible contributors to poor health outcomes among persons living with HIV/AIDS. This dissertation explores the relationships between food insecurity, perceived HIV stigma, and health outcomes among low-income Oklahomans receiving treatment for HIV/AIDS. A mixed-methods research approach included the administration of standardized surveys (N = 164) and a series of four focus group discussions (N = 31) among low-income, HIV-positive persons living in eastern and western Oklahoma. Research findings revealed that food insecurity is highly prevalent among low-income Oklahomans receiving treatment for HIV/AIDS, regardless of geographic region or case management provider. Despite frequent use of food assistance programs, the experience of food insecurity is nearly universal among this clinical population, with nearly nine out of ten persons experiencing some aspect of food insecurity in the past year. Additionally, food insecure Oklahomans receiving treatment for HIV/AIDS experience greater degrees of perceived HIV stigma, more frequent mental distress, and lower self-rated physical health. These findings suggest that food insecurity plays a fundamental role in the perceived mental and physical well-being of members within this population. In order for food insecurity to be improved, significant changes must be made to the current system of food assistance for low-income persons living with HIV/AIDS. [Author Abstract]

156.) **Whitley, S.**

Changing times in rural America: The effects on food insecurity and hunger.

Ph.D. dissertation, Washington State University. 2012.

Poverty and hunger are increasingly significant issues facing the nation, in large part due to an economic recession that began in 2007 and ended in 2009 (National Bureau of Economic Research), but the consequences of which still remain apparent (Bean 2011). One result of rising hunger rates is the increasing number of public assistance caseloads for the Supplemental Nutrition Assistance Program (SNAP) (Bean 2011), however, as Americans experience economic distress they are also looking to community programs for additional and needed services, such as food pantries which offer unprepared food items (Berner et al. 2008; Biggerstaff et al. 2002; Daponte et al. 2004; Molnar et al. 2001; Nnakwe 2008). Yet researchers have relatively little data on the hunger struggles of this extremely vulnerable population, especially in the rural setting and in the West where it has been suggested poverty and hunger rates are higher than in other regions (Farrigan 2010; Nord et al. 2009). Using qualitative interviews and ethnographic fieldwork, the current study tells a story about who the rural food insecure are in Perry County, Washington, and how they survive each month while experiencing significant changes in the rural environment. The study argues that the needs of pantry users vary across locations and between individuals using the same pantry. The study also tells an important story of how rural food insecure diets are affected by retail access changes. From a spatial inequality perspective, access changes have negatively affected rural residents' food security for a variety of reasons that seem unique to the rural setting. The changes taking place in Perry County are important to evaluate because they mirror changes happening across the country in the rural setting. At a time when hunger is hitting our nation at an alarming rate, it is important to have a better understanding of who faces food insecurity and the challenges those individuals and food programs endure combating hunger issues. [Author Abstract]

157.) **Wilber, K. R.**

Measurement of the impact of home delivered meals on food insecurity in the elderly population.

M.S. thesis, D'Youville College. 2012.

The purpose of this study was to determine if home delivered meal programs had an impact on the food security of elderly homebound recipients. The subjects (n = 22) participated in phone interviews to measure their level of food security (before receiving and while receiving services from the meal programs) using the USDA Adult Food Security Module. The t- test was used to find pre-/post-test differences in the level of food security. The home delivered meal programs had a significant impact (p = 0.0044) on the recipient's food security level. Fifty percent of the subjects reported increased food security levels and none had a decrease in food security levels. This study found that home delivered meal programs reduce senior's food insecurity. [Author Abstract]

158.) **Willis, D.**

Resources and Relationships: Food Insecurity and Social Capital among Middle School Students.

M.A. thesis, University of Arkansas. 2013.

This study examines the relationship between food insecurity and social capital among 5th-7th graders attending an intermediate school in Northwest Arkansas where nearly 70 percent of students participate in the free or reduced lunch program. The central research questions are: Does social capital have a direct impact on children's food insecurity? And, does social capital mediate the influence of negative circumstances on children's food insecurity? This study finds that social capital does have a significant association with food insecurity, even when controlling for multiple demographic and circumstantial factors. However, there appears to be no mediation of circumstance by social capital. Additionally, we find that the quality of relationships among peers, rather than the quantity of close friends, plays a primary role in children's food insecurity. Together, these findings tell a story about the importance of relationships among middle-school children and how these connections may function to provide a shield from insecurity. More broadly, however, this study informs the larger question of how hunger exists in a nation as rich as the United States by addressing food insecurity as a social phenomenon rather than simply an economic, technological, or biological one. [Author Abstract]

159.) **Wogene, T. W.**

Infant recognition memory and physical growth in Wolayita: Relations to maternal depression, food insecurity social support and mother-infant interaction.

Ph.D. dissertation, Oklahoma State University. 2012.

Scope and Method of Study: The purpose of the study was to assess relations of maternal depression (Edinburgh Postnatal Depression Scale, EPDS), food insecurity, social support, maternal nutrition status (BMI), maternal education, family economic resources, and perceived social status with mother-infant interaction and infant weight-for-age (WAZ), length-for-age (LAZ), weight-for-length (WLZ), and recognition memory. In phase I, mother-infant dyads (N =201) were recruited by convenience sampling in Wolayita, Southern Ethiopia. Maternal depression, stressful life events, food insecurity, social support, demographic variables, and maternal weight and height and infant weight and length were measured. In phase II, 83 mother-infant dyads were recruited from the phase I sample; attrition reduced the sample to 73 (n =34 with EPDS $\leq$ 12 and n =39 with EPDS $\geq$ 14). Mother-infant interaction was videotaped and infant cognitive skills, look duration (information processing speed) and recognition memory (novelty preference) were measured. Findings and Conclusions: Main findings were (1) Continuous EPDS scores measuring maternal depression were not directly associated with infant growth. Food insecurity, β= -.215, p 18.5 or more social support, EPDS was not related to weight or length. For infants of mothers with BMI < 18.5, EPDS was significantly negatively related to WAZ and LAZ; for infants of mothers with low social support, EPDS was significantly negatively related to WAZ and WLZ. (3) EPDS scores categorized from low to high depressive symptoms were significantly negatively related to maternal positive affect in interactions. (4) Lower maternal depression and higher maternal positive affect were associated with faster infant information processing but infant underweight status was associated with poorer recognition memory. Results are interpreted as reconciling previous inconsistent findings. [Author Abstract]

160.) **Yasak, E. W.**

Poverty and food insecurity in the Democratic Republic of the Congo.

M.A. thesis, Michigan State University. 2002.

Food insecurity and poverty in the Democratic Republic of Congo (DRC) have been explained by both national and international factors. We assume that food insecurity is caused primarily by lack of democracy and unequal distribution of resources, especially land and income. The lack of democracy, the poor management, and lack of accountability by Congolese leaders are some factors sustaining and perpetuating poverty and food insecurity in the DRC. At the national and local level, there is a great need to educate Congolese people to shift away from the traditional practices that perpetuate gender inequality, poverty, hunger, and food insecurity. At the global levels, a study is needed on the conditions for aid for development. The cutting spending on social programs might perpetuate poverty. It is concluded that DRC needs modernization of agriculture, food storage facilities, and transportation system connecting rural areas to cities within the country and with neighboring African countries. Investing in rural areas by improving the infrastructure such as road, schools, hospitals, bridges, solar energy, water systems are needed if DRC wants to alleviate poverty and address food insecurity issues. The lack of job creation and peace in DRC have undermined the prospects for poverty reduction. [Author Abstract]

161.) **Ye, Q.**

Food Insecurity and Obesity in Low-Income Women: The Monthly Cycle of Food Abundance and Food Shortage.

Ph.D. dissertation, The Ohio State University. 2011.

Food insecurity has been associated with overweight/obesity in U.S. women. Several hypotheses have been proposed to address this paradoxical association, but none has yet been tested. This dissertation is designed to test the "monthly cycle of food abundance and food shortage" hypothesis, and to examine the effects of food stamp program (FSP) participation, disordered eating, and dietary intake patterns on the association. It is hypothesized that food insecure women would experience a monthly cycle with higher total energy intake (TEI) and household food stores at the beginning of the month, followed by a more limited TEI and food supply at the end. The dissertation compared food insecure and overweight/obese (FIS/ovob) women with three other women groups: food secure and normal weight (FS/norm), food secure and overweight/obese (FS/ovob), and food insecure and normal weight (FIS/norm). The monthly variations in TEI and food stores were assessed in a sample of low-income women in Ohio, by comparing the energy intake from the first ten days with that of the last ten days of the month during three continuous months. For FIS/ovob women, significant decreases were found in the total number of food items (Month 1: 87.74 vs. 68.26, Month 2: 83.3 vs. 72.2, Month 3: 88.81 vs. 75.3, $p<0.05$) and in essential food groups including grains, vegetables, fruits, meat & beans, and milk; in TEI (2114.19 vs. 1843.06 kcal, $p<0.05$) and fat intake (804.1 vs. 649.93 kcal, $p<0.05$) in Month 1. Among food insecure women, food stamp recipients showed a higher BMI (38.24 vs. 30.94, $p<0.01$) and more severe decreases in three-month food items (61.58 vs. 8.22, $p<0.01$) than non-recipients. In addition, deeper food insecurity was marginally correlated with more severe Eating Concern in disordered eating (Pearson's correlation: 0.23, $p=0.09$). Using the National Health and Nutrition Examination Survey (NHANES) 1999-2008 data, a higher carbohydrates/energy ratio and a lower protein/energy ratio was found in FIS/ovob women compared to food secure women; no differences of TEI or fat/energy ratio were observed. Furthermore, FIS/ovob women showed higher prevalence of a 4.54 kg (10 lbs) 1-yr weight gain (28.81%) than other women groups. The results suggest the existence of the monthly cycle of food abundance and food shortage in FIS/ovob women, which may be caused by the interaction in food insecurity with FSP participation; carbohydrate intake may increase, and daily energy intake and fat intake may fluctuate in response to the monthly cycle and result in gradual weight gain over long periods of time. Policy changes may be necessary; nutrition education integrating with community-based intervention programs and efforts from private sectors like food providers are needed for FIS/ovob women to have a more even distribution of available food sources throughout the month, and a reduction of the potentially episodic overeating behaviors. [Author Abstract]

162.) **Yoshikawa, N.**

Untying the Gordian knot: A consideration of the effects of aid in Asia and the Pacific. Ph.D. dissertation, University of Hawai'i. 1999.

This paper discusses the social effects of foreign aid (both bilateral--especially U.S. and Japanese aid--and multilateral development aid) in the Asia-Pacific region. Foreign aid is often criticized as contributing to social and economic deterioration rather than improvement in many aid recipient countries. This research examines the aid process in depth, and, using qualitative and quantitative methods, identifies those factors which account for adverse consequences in aid recipient societies. The detrimental effects of aid are assessed by three variables: poverty increase, gender inequality and food insecurity in the aid recipient society. It is possible to envisage that the aid donor overlooked the detrimental effects of its foreign assistance on the aid recipient countries in order to pursue its own economic and/or political benefits in some cases. However, consideration of donor's interests in the aid process does not explain all the adverse effects of aid since similar types of aid had different effects in different recipient countries. For example, the same type of development project aid, which provided technology to increase agriculture production, improved conditions for the majority in some countries and worsened conditions for the majority in other countries. The results of both qualitative and quantitative analyses confirm that the detrimental effects of aid are due not only to the "manner of giving" of donors but also largely to the "manner of receiving" aid, which is conditioned by the political and social situation of the aid recipient country. Relevant factors in this regard include government unaccountable to the majority and unresponsive to the majority, corruption, political instability, etc. Whether aid can be fully utilized for improving the lives of the majority in the recipient country or aid is used to benefit a small elite in the country is mostly determined by the recipient country itself. Aid could be a catalyst for amplifying the detrimental social conditions for the majority in the aid recipient country, but it is not the "permissive" cause of adverse effects of aid itself. [Author Abstract]

163.) **Zarb, N.**

Protracted conflict and food insecurity in Africa case studies of Democratic Republic of the Congo and Somalia.

M.S. thesis, George Mason University. 2011.

Food insecurity exists when people do not have adequate physical, social or economic access to food. This impacts millions of lives every day and often times countries that are food insecure have populations that are more likely to live below the international poverty line. Although the international community is committed to halving the proportion of people suffering from malnutrition from 1990-2015, the efforts to accomplish this goal have been limited and is still significantly far away from its target. Africa suffers immensely from food insecurity; the prevalence of conflict makes it difficult to address the problem because the violence results in fragmented communities, instability, and individuals leaving their homes to find alternate food solutions. This in turn results in lowered food production due to an inability to cultivate the land because it is either too unsafe to do so or because the land has been abandoned. Subsequently, due to lowered food production African countries' economies are negatively impacted because agriculture accounts for a large proportion of their gross domestic product and employment. As a result of a lowered production rate, the dependence on international aid increases. In some cases, violence and food insecurity have become commonplace and organisations have failed to resolve the issue for decades. If the goal to reduce and eventually eradicate global hunger is to be achieved, it is necessary that food insecurity and conflict are properly dealt with. Humanitarian organisations must go beyond shortterm response mechanisms and implement long-term measures as well. Even though some countries may have achieved positive peace after conflict has ceased, it is not guaranteed that food security will result and that future grievances may not be expressed. It is imperative that organisations commit to assisting countries to achieve stability, transparent governments, and productive economies so as to avoid future occurrences of food insecurity and conflict. This study assesses the relationship between protracted conflict and food security in Africa. By assessing the factors that contribute to conflict and weaken a country's food security, it was found that there is a direct correlation between the two factors however it is not guaranteed that food insecurity will result in conflict. The study analyses the response mechanisms that have been adopted by international organisations and evaluates their effectiveness at addressing the immediate problems and long-term consequences associated with conflict and insecurity. The Democratic Republic of the Congo and Somalia are case studies that are used to examine the impacts of food security as a result of conflict. Both countries demonstrate how a lack of functioning, transparent government and prevalence of violence throughout the country severely impacts people's lives and accessibility to food which results in mass displacement. This makes it extremely difficult for humanitarian organisations to implement response mechanisms to improve the livelihoods of individuals, and while immediate food aid is helpful, it is only a temporary response. In order to properly address protracted conflict and food insecurity, it is necessary that humanitarian organisations develop response mechanisms that address immediate food needs as well as help to reduce the prevalence of conflict. In addition, it has proven to be beneficial to take into consideration other factors that are impacted as a result of conflict and food insecurity; addressing gender needs as well as ensuring access to education have both proven to significantly improve individuals' livelihoods. Ensuring that these needs are addressed will help reduce the prevalence of food insecurity and conflict in the world and also help to work towards the other Millennium Development Goals to improve the lives of the world's poorest. This requires long-term commitment on the part of international organisations that are willing to ensure that the symptoms that result in protracted conflict and food insecurity are properly dealt with. Otherwise, there lies the risk of cyclical outbreaks of violence and food insecurity which negatively impacts individuals' livelihoods and moves further away from achieving the goal of eradicating world hunger. [Author Abstract]

Locating Dissertations and Theses

A. Purchase

Many of the dissertations and theses listed in this bibliography are available for purchase through UMI Dissertation Express:

http://disexpress.umi.com/dxweb

By Fax:

800-864-0019

By Mail:

789 E. Eisenhower Parkway, P.O. Box 1346, Ann Arbor, Michigan 48106-1346

800-521-3042

B. Interlibrary Loan

Dissertations and theses may also be requested through Interlibrary Loan via your local public, college or university library.

www.ingramcontent.com/pod-product-compliance
Lightning Source LLC
Chambersburg PA
CBHW080407290526
45791CB00008BA/2177

9781515242826